Youth Empowerment in the Church

Youth Empowerment in the Church

A Handbook for Youth Ministry

Brenda Gorrell Pyatt

Youth Ministry Resource

Published for the Youth Staff Team
Joint Educational Development
by United Church Press
New York

Joint Education Development—an ecumenical partnership for the development of educational systems and resources: Christian Church (Disciples of Christ), Church of the Brethren, Cumberland Presbyterian Church, The Episcopal Church, The Evangelical Covenant Church, Moravian Church in America, Presbyterian Church in Canada, Presbyterian Church in the United States, Reformed Church in America, United Church of Canada, United Church of Christ, United Presbyterian Church in the USA.

Editor: Audrey Miller
Copy Editor: Carol McCollough
Designer: Robert Koenig

Library of Congress Cataloging in Publication Data

Pyatt, Brenda Gorrell, 1952–
   Youth empowerment in the church.

   "A Youth Ministry Resource."
   1. Church work with youth—Handbooks, manuals, etc.
I. Title.
BV4447.P9 1983   259′.23   82-23851
ISBN 0-8298-0605-9 (pbk.)

United Church Press, 132 W. 31 Street, New York, NY 10001

To Bill, Dan, Lorin, Kevin, and Herman
—for being there and sharing yourselves
and teaching me so much.

Contents

Preface

It has been a practical adventure that brings you *Youth Empowerment in the Church*. The practicality of this venture is in its utility. This handbook is the report of what actually happened and what can be done. We do not mean to ignore or disparage the helpful, more theoretical and philosophical books on youth and ministry. We acknowledge them and are grateful for their influence in the creation and implementation of youth ministry. This book, however, is a report of what happened and is happening, with suggestions and guidelines for your use.

Youth empowerment is a full-fledged adventure that has occurred in several different parts of the country, tested by several different denominations, both independently and ecumenically. It is an adventure in various kinds of teams: all young people, youth and young adults, city youth and country youth, Black youth and white youth, young men and young women.

Likewise, the writing of this book has been an adventure. Instead of the typical well established author, we placed the task of retelling and re-arranging the many reports into the hands of a young adult, Brenda Gorrell Pyatt. Brenda brought to this task intimate and extensive experience. As a young person in Ohio, Brenda was a member of the original Youth Empowerment Team. After a two-year stint there, she provided leadership training for youth teams in Ohio and Georgia as a youth consultant for the United Church Board for Homeland Ministries. Brenda knows of what she speaks when she presents to us vignettes of existing teams and suggestions for activities and reflections.

Together with Brenda, we, the JED Youth Empowerment Project Team, invite you to join the continuation of this adventure. Welcome and God speed you as you journey with youth in ministry teams for empowerment.

JED Youth Empowerment Project
Audrey Miller, United Church of Christ
   Editor and Project Director
Elizabeth Crawford, Episcopal Church
   Project Member
Jerry Befus, Moravian Church of America
   Project Member

Introduction

Youth Empowerment was a new concept in ministry when Joint Educational Development (JED) decided to develop experimental models inspired by it. JED is a partnership of twelve denominations working together on various ministries in Christian education, youth ministry and other educational ministries. Because many tasks can be done better by pooling our resources, working ecumenically, and sharing our discoveries; professionals from these denominations cooperate in exploring, developing, and carrying out new forms of educational ministry. The learnings from these projects are made available through denominational channels or, as in this case to a wider public, through a denominational press.

What can happen when young people minister to and with one another and work toward becoming a part of the whole church today? JED initiated several projects to find out. Most of these projects were variations of what was developed originally as the Youth Empowerment Team.

The JED Youth Empowerment Team discovered some exciting things about youth ministry, youth empowerment, young people working with adults and other young people.

Youth empowerment teams work at strengthening youth leadership as well as developing a communication and resource network for local churches and judicatories.[1] Because of the need to enhance the presence of young people in the ministries of the church and to bring the perspective, vision, voice, and vote of young people into the policy-making and program-forming structures of the church, teams of youth and young adults were hired to develop and implement ways to make this happen.

Seattle, Washington was the site of the first Youth Empowerment Team (YET) planned and supported by Joint Educational Development. The learnings from this team were put to use in the development of a second Team in Georgia. Spin-off projects in several denominations were based on the learnings from these two projects.

Youth empowerment is just one of the many tracks that youth ministry can take. It can give young people a chance to be leaders and decision-makers, to be enablers, to grow actively in their faith, and to spread the good news. It is based on the attitude that young people have the ability to be leaders and are capable and competent to be full participants in the Christian community.

Youth empowerment is not young people marching to storm the podium at the church's annual meeting, taking over, and declaring their views. Youth empowerment *is* rather a move to stimulate the participation of young people in the life of their church. It is enabling the voice of youth to be among the chorus of viewpoints. It is youth helping youth and adults develop their skills and grow in their faith. It is adults and youth working together.

The major purpose for this book is to share with you the outlines of several different youth empowerment models. Looking at the styles, the goals, the similarities, the differences, the learnings and the spin-offs, you will see the many faces of youth empowerment at work. Through reflecting on these models and adapting the planning process and designs to your situation you can use this book as a guide for developing your own youth empowerment model in the local church or judicatory.

Various chapters will discuss youth empowerment, give examples of learnings from some specific youth empowerment models, and explore how youth empowerment can work for you. An outline for a planning process will give the steps for planning your own form of youth empowerment. Some thoughts about leadership, training, evaluation, and celebration will help you to put that plan into action. A resource listing will help to expand your plans creatively.

One suggestion for using this book more effectively is: Don't only read it, do it. In most chapters there are suggestions for "journal jottings" that will help you to focus on your own thoughts and feelings about youth ministry and empowerment. Each exercise is to give you time and impetus to do your own reflecting. It is to your advantage to work through this book as you read it. But no matter how you do it, this book is for:

- You, the youth or young adult concerned about youth ministry in your local church.
- You, the adult advocate for a local youth group.
- You, the pastor who wants youth to be involved.
- You, the person who wants to get activities started or revitalized for youth and youth leaders of your judicatory or ecumenical cluster.
- You, the young person who wants to enable the empowerment of other young people in and through the church.

Welcome to this book! It is for you.

Note

1. Judicatory: A designated regional body of a denomination composed of a group of churches working together programmatically in a geographical area.

Part 1

Youth Empowerment —Who?

CHAPTER ONE

These Christians Called Youth

It would be presumptuous to write a book on youth ministry without a background of experiences with young people in ministry. It would be equally questionable to read it without a sense of the context of young people. Definitions of youth and ministry are created out of the experiences with young people in ministry. Youth ministry is not an objective topic. It is immensely subjective, built on the people who make it up. Many books provide scientific and theoretical information on young people and their development. This will not be a repetition of that information. It is important and helpful to be familiar with these theories. But it is equally important to reflect on your experiences and recognize the attitudes and perceptions you have internalized. Take a minute now to identify your experiences and reflections on young people.

Journal Jottings:

A Young Person is . . .

Begin your exploration by jotting down those adjectives that come to your mind when you are asked to describe the young people you know—your friends, peers, pupils, those in your church, at your community center, on your judicatory task force. Who are they? What are they like? Write down those descriptions which are true to the range of your experience. When you have finished writing, keep the paper or journal you are using within reach. Add to it if more feelings or ideas come to mind as you read on.

The most important factors in your youth ministry are the characteristics of your situation and the young people and adults with whom you are involved. Youth ministry is a process that includes many interrelated aspects. There are general learnings, views, and ways of working and interacting that can be applied at different times with varying success. How these actions take effect is dependent on your Christian community. So as you jot down your thoughts and feelings about youth, keep in mind, for example: Alicia, who is shy, but has the potential to be a good leader; Jack, who is great at building fires on campouts, but finds it difficult to share his feelings; Jan, who tends to do all the work of the committee herself; and Marty, the frustrated idealist. These are your young people for ministry. Who are they?

Young People and the Church

Just as you, the reader, need to develop your own understanding of the young people with whom you work, it is necessary to present in this initial chapter those feelings, assumptions and affirmations about young people which are the foundation of this book and the model of youth ministry contained in it.

Young people are valuable members of the church today. A deceptively simple statement. Behind these few words are

4

packed several attitudes about youth which describe more precisely what these words mean.

"Young people are valuable" implies that the viewpoint of young people on all issues is important in forming a total picture for decision making within the church. It says that youth are creative, intelligent, faithful people, capable of being and becoming leaders. And it says that youth have the capacity for empowering leadership, creativity, and Christian awareness in others.

"Young people are . . . members" states that churches must recognize the gap that exists if young people are not an active part of their community. The church must risk new ways of operating to fill this gap. Only in this way can churches celebrate the wholeness that comes when the body of Christ works, loves and grows together.

"Young people are . . . the church today." To make this concept a reality, young people must have the chance to practice and test their skills. They need an opportunity to experience leadership in their own youth groups, in their local churches, and in judicatory structures. Also they must have the freedom to grow in their faith within a community of support.

"Young people are valuable members of the church today". This statement is the basic understanding of the youth empowerment model portrayed in this book. It is the essential premise on which to build a viable youth ministry.

In our ministry of the church we first need to discover and to define our own concept of what that ministry should be.

• What is its purpose?
• What are the possibilities?
• Who will it be affecting?
• What are their needs?

These are only a few of the questions you should start asking yourself about youth ministry and yourself. Youth empowerment is just one of the models of youth ministry. It can best be explored by first looking at the total ministry of your church.

Three aspects must be explored and brought together as you are formulating your definition of youth ministry:

- The needs, concerns, and interests of the young people who are a part of that ministry.
- The church's role and ministry to young people and to the world. This includes both its mission and the values, attitudes and actions which it lives out.
- The challenge and guidance that the scriptures bring to us as Christian ministers.

You have already started by looking at the young people you know. Now let's look at the church.

Journal Jottings II

The church is . . .

Look at the sheet where you have been writing your adjectives and descriptive phrases about young people. What have you recorded so far?

What new thoughts have been triggered by what you have read? Write those down.

Take out another page and head it, "The church is . . .". Finish this sentence with several phrases of your own experiences and beliefs. Then expand on this by listing important issues you feel the church should face in the world today.

At a retreat center in Georgia several high school young people gathered recently to discuss their thoughts about the church. The following lists reflect their feelings about important issues the church today needs to face. They cross quite a wide range of issues and indicate a general consensus that a church's ministry should touch all facets of our society. As you read this list, compare it to your list of issues.

Honesty	Stereotypes
Crisis	Overpopulation
Abortion	Human welfare
Friends to the	and human
friendless	rights
Rehabilitation	Tolerance
for criminals	Authority
Unemployment	Poverty
Sex and violence	Human sexuality
on television	Equal Rights
How to be a	Drug abuse
Christian in	Alcoholism
the crowd	Energy
Life and death	Self-Awareness
Social	Communication
relationships	Ecumenicity
Money	Divorce
Orphans	Unity

These young people also spent a great deal of time searching within themselves and the scriptures to determine the meaning of ministry. Recalling actions and events which had influenced their lives, they identified many values and attitudes which were important to them and which they wanted to include in their ministry. Concern, love, trust, hard work, common sense, patience, dedication, openness, gentleness, perseverance, honesty, self-reliance, sensitivity, and acceptance were some of the values that had been part of someone's ministry to them. What about your life?

7

Journal Jottings III

Values for Ministry

Consider the times when someone has ministered to you. What were the attitudes and values which made those interactions beneficial and worth remembering? Why were those moments special? On one side of your sheet list some values which are important to your ministry.

The scriptures are a treasury of thoughts on ministry—for example, Luke 4:16–30 and John 13:4–17. Examine the parables for accounts of people ministering to one another. Read them aloud. Act them out. Imagine yourself as each of the characters. Become involved in discovering the concept of ministry which Jesus described to eager listeners. Who were called? How did they respond? How can we respond?

Journal Jottings IV

Ministry in the Bible

Open the Bible to one of your favorite passages. Read it. What does it convey about ministry? Now try these: 1 Corinthians 12:4–16, 27; Ephesians 4:11–16; I Peter 2:9–10; Luke 4:16–19. These all say something about us as Christians. What do they challenge us to do? As youth? As adults? As a local church? As a task force concerned about youth ministry? Reflect on each one of these passages. In what ways can we meet these challenges? Write down some of the challenges you feel these words are calling you to do.

Consider the thoughts and feelings about ministry which surfaced as you have explored the three aspects of youth, ministry, and scripture. Reflect on their interac-

tion. Bring your ideas together as you formulate your
own definition of youth ministry.

Journal Jottings V

Youth plus Ministry

Look back over the three areas which you have explored
in the previous exercises; the youth with whom you are
involved, their needs and interests; the mission of the
church in the world today, and the values and attitudes
which the church should live out in its ministry; and the
challenge of the scriptures to Christian ministers. As you
look at all of these, how do they shape your thoughts of
youth ministry? Write your definition of youth ministry.

Several high school students from Georgia, Alabama, and
Tennessee defined youth ministry in the following ways:

"Youth ministry is showing youth how they can be involved
with the work of Christ in conjunction with helping others
seek and find contentment."

"Youth ministry is striving together for the total involvement of young people and adults in order to show love,
growth in justice and deepening of faith."

"Listening, learning, teaching, understanding, and meeting
the needs of others through just love and growing together in
faith in God."

"It is drawing strength, wisdom and guidance from Christ to
cope with and find solutions to problems that are already here,
and prevent those problems that may be around tomorrow."

"Trying to deepen [my own] and others' faith. Understand-

9

ing someone's problem without judging him or putting him down because of his problem. Have an open mind; try to look at things as God would; learn to listen and listen to learn! Have a total involvement in your youth group."

"Kids who are becoming interested in other people and the world around them are starting to care and reach out to help those in need. They are coming together, learning to be leaders, and are reaching out to other young people. They are becoming interested in the problems of our world and setting out to do something about it."

These definitions touch on the spectrum of youth ministry; the whole spectrum of reaching out to others, loving and helping those in need, learning about God and the Christian faith, having total involvement in the church, demonstrating active concern about social issues, sharing ourselves and our riches with others, and fulfilling the mandates of the Gospel. They reflect the feelings of those young people. Your definition should reflect you and those with whom you are building your ministry.

A church's ministry to and with its young people is one of the most vital and dynamic, creative and exciting, tiring and confusing, fun and freeing, caring and demanding, liberating and uniting ministries that can happen. To be involved within that ministry can carry you through joys, worries, pancake breakfasts, potluck suppers, celebrations, commission meetings, simulations, small groups, study groups, annual meetings, leadership training events, canoe trips, and car washes. Nothing else is quite like it.

Those who are called are concerned about young people and their place in the church today. If you are one of those people, then this book is for you because it tells the stories of other people who are too.

Notes

1. Carol Blakely, "Give Us Room To Grow," *Youth Magazine*. Volume 29, Number 2, February, 1978.
2. Chas Elicker, *Journey Without Maps*. United Church Press, Philadelphia, 1976. (P. 114.)
3. Carl S. Southerland, "Youth Empowerment Teams: An Experiment," *The North American Moravian*. July–August, 1978.
4. Blakely, ibid., pp. 13–16.

CHAPTER TWO

Youth Empowerment
in Words and Lives

Youth ministry encompasses the people, places and experiences which touch young people as they grow in their Christian faith and in the church community. Youth empowerment is both a form and a style of youth ministry.

Youth empowerment is that unique form of ministry which says that young people are capable of being leaders, planners, and decision makers. This ministry affirms the skills, talents, viewpoints, and insights of youth. It says that they are needed to complete and fulfill what the church is called to do. Youth empowerment activates the well worn phrase which tells us that youth are not only the future of the church, they are the church today.

Incorporating young people into the total life of the church, locally, regionally, and denominationally is where youth empowerment starts. It begins with the church recognizing the need to hear the voice of all ages in its family and to perform its ministry in response to that chorus of voices.

12

An ecumenical example of just such an effort was developed in Georgia. Three young adults were hired full time and one adult part-time to bring greater involvement of youth in the churches of Georgia. Titled the *Georgia Youth Empowerment Team*, the young adults traveled in designated areas of Georgia working with local churches and judicatory groups of the United Church of Christ, the Christian Church (Disciples of Christ), and the Episcopal Church. They found the reaction to youth empowerment to be quite startling. Says Carol Blakely, one team member:

> The team's ministry primarily involved helping young people to recognize, to claim, and begin to put to work their full potential." Cassandra Young, another team member comments, "I will readily admit that our ideas were a bit revolutionary for some. We had seen for ourselves the restrained role with which youth are sometimes confined, in contrast to an atmosphere where youth are accepted as equal partners among fellow church members. The transition from tokenism to full participation in the church can be considered nothing less than revolutionary and is successful only where a God of love and justice gently inspires the change.[1]

The term Youth Empowerment can be somewhat intimidating. It may bring to mind thoughts of uppity young people, the church being rent assunder and bitter conflict. But that is not what Youth Empowerment is about.

Youth Empowerment is a process:

> Young people recognizing that they have a stake in the church,
> Young people beginning to learn who they are and where they hope the church will go,
> Young people sharing their ideas and strength to help

shape the decisions that will guide the future of the church.

Youth Empowerment is the process of becoming full participants in the Christian community."[2]

This is the basic premise of another Youth Empowerment Team, based in Seattle, and sponsored by a joint ministry of the Christian Church (Disciples of Christ), the Church of the Brethren, and the United Church of Christ. A team of two young adults traveled over twenty-six thousand miles working with local churches and judicatory groups in Washington state and northern Idaho. They worked with both youth and adults of local churches and judicatories in communication skills, personal valuing, planning, organizing and leadership development.

Other Youth Empowerment Teams (YET) have been sponsored by several individual denominations. Though bearing the same or similar titles, these projects have all taken different shapes.

The Moravian Church in North America, for example, has had several Youth Empowerment Teams composed of high school students. Working in the southern part of the United States and in Canada, these teams of five young people each had as their goals "enhancing youth ministry in the local congregations, enabling team members to provide peer leadership training, and raising the awareness in churches of the need for youth involvement in the total life of the church. As part of their task, one team worked with eighteen local congregations, led a provincial youth ministry workshop, and designed and led a senior high weekend experience. One team member Joyce Carter, described her experience this way:

Now, because of YET, I became part of an exciting task; helping youth to set goals and dreams, so that their youth ministry program might be strengthened. As a result . . .

14

my knowledge and concern have increased greatly, and my faith has been strengthened to the point where I want to share it.[3]

Another team, working in the Ohio Conference of the United Church of Christ, employed four young adults to work full time in resourcing local churches and area youth task forces. Said one team member:

"Before I joined the Youth Empowerment Team, I never realized that there were things happening for youth beyond my local church youth group. My year in the YET showed me broad new dimensions of the church that I had never known before. I was enriched just by meeting and getting to know those people who were active in the Association and in the Conference. My faith was strengthened, and I grew in pride and respect for my denomination and what it does. I only wish that I had learned all this when I was in high school so that I could have taken part in all those youth rallies and retreats that were happening then.

Youth Empowerment Teams are beneficial, not only for those youth in local churches with whom they work, but for those youth and young adults who constitute the core team. Carol Blakely was a member of the Georgia Youth Empowerment Team, and described her experiences in an article which appeared in *Youth Magazine*. This article pulls together sensitively and concisely what Youth Empowerment Teams are. Part of Carol's article follows:

Give Us Room to Grow

For fifteen months, a team of originally three and then two young adults toured the state of Georgia under the title of the Georgia Youth Empowerment Team (GYET) visiting youth and local churches.

The youth ministry of the team as outlined by Joint

Educational Development involved three primary areas of concentration: first, and most importantly, empowerment of the individual taking place as youth come to recognize their own value as human beings; second, empowerment of youth in the church, collectively demonstrating an increased involvement; and third, empowerment of the body of believers through clusters of churches united together to combine resource materials and persons, thereby, improving programs and overall ministry. Underlying each of these areas were basic concepts adapted by the team.

In order for everyone to grow, we must know that someone believes in us and cares about our progress. The Georgia team members attempted to let each young person know that he or she was one of God's uniquely created beings with individual strengths and weaknesses; no better and no worse than the next person but an equal partner in the adventures of life. . . .

Empowerment takes place when persons—young and old—come to believe in themselves. In this day and age of constant criticism and frantic struggle to be the person on the top and "part of the crowd", we attempt to hide our doubts about ourselves. One of the most effective ways for these insecurities to become less fearful is through sharing them with a group of supportive people.

In the Team's work with church youth groups, attempts were executed to create in each group a supportive Christian community demonstrating the following characteristics: Youth feel accepted as they are and trust one another enough to be open and honest, removing the masks that each of us wears. . . . Each member feels supported by others, enabling each to overcome his or her fears and reach out to a deeper, understanding of oneself and an establishment of a strengthened commitment to the church.

Sound like an impossible group? Certainly you will never be able to maintain this type of supportive group continuously, but various levels of it are possible and are happening in youth groups.

Those adults who are involved in youth ministry, or advocates for youth, as they are sometimes called, are often frustrated when attempting to achieve this type of community. A few suggestions for them: Don't give up. Your support and direction are crucial. . . . Don't "do for" the youth; let them learn on their own. Your role in establishing a mood of openness is key—be ready to share openly and honestly and the youth will do the same in return. Affirm others and you'll be affirmed.

[Another] concept [of these] excitingly radical changes involves the realization of the following: The youth of the church are not only the church of tomorrow, as everyone claims, but they are also essential for the proper functioning of the body of Christ today. The youth of a church may be blessed with a unique ability to hear and listen to the cries of the world around them. Or they may be the eyes of the body really seeing the desperate needs of the community that the rest of us are too blind to see. Or they may be the legs with the energy and the willpower to act on needs which others have observed. In the agony of growth, youth are sensitive to varieties of pain. In their untested idealism, they are a refreshing conscience. Young in body and spirit, they are eager and impatient for action.

Whatever the role, each youth in the church has a gift or talent that when used will benefit the total church. The idea of empowerment, therefore, is related to active involvement—wholehearted involvement of youth spiritually, mentally, and physically for the benefit of the church today and tomorrow.

Why aren't more churches recognizing youth as an important part of the body of Christ and why aren't more youth accepting the responsibility which goes along with increased involvement? Two attitudes could be the explanation. . . .

First, the church could just not care about their young people. Their attentions are directed to other areas of ministry and the youth are a low priority. The youth, in return, will certainly be unwilling to make a real commitment to a group of people who are not interested in them. If there is no commitment on the part of the young person, then he or she can easily be drawn away from the church to innumerable other ways of spending his or her time. When this happens, the total church suffers because an important part of it is not participating.

On the other hand, the church could care about its young people, but not know how to direct that attention. Over-zealous adults attempting to dictate the actions of the young people have a similar effect of turning the young people off from the life of the church. What is the answer? Communication and acceptance. Between the adults and young people, communication lines must remain open to share needs and to offer support. Evening rap sessions where adults and youth divide into small groups for discussions on a prearranged subject or a subject decided on by the group are an excellent means of bridging the "generation gap". Such opportunities for dialogue should be provided on a regular basis in every church. . . .

What could happen if this idea of empowerment became a reality within your church? On a local level, youth working towards having representation on all the decision-making committees of the church is just one aspect. This representation would allow youth to speak out concerning their beliefs, their needs, and their support, all for the benefit of the total church.

Participation in the already-established, decision-making bodies on the state and national levels is also an important facet of youth empowerment. Youth are capable of writing responsible proposals and speaking out reasonably on their opinions of current issues. This has happened in Georgia. But this can happen only as youth reach out further than the narrow boundaries they have set for themselves.

Does empowerment still sound like a revolutionary concept? Work towards making it a reality within your life and the lives of the other youth of your church. Maybe it will spread to the rest of the congregation. We all . . . no matter what our age, need to be empowered. Always remember that our Christian gospel is really a revolutionary idea, even though it has been in existence for over a thousand years. We are called to be instigators of change, but always in love. Listen and act as God speaks to you through the Word of God and through others. Know that God loves you and watch God transform your life and lives of the people of the Church.[4]

For these thoughts, dreams and affirmations of youth empowerment to be a reality, they need the time and hard work of those people—youth and adults—who believe it can happen. Youth empowerment teams were created and supported in order to enable the process of empowerment to take place. A more in-depth look at the Georgia Youth Empowerment Team (GYET) model can give a better understanding of nuts and bolts which build youth empowerment.

First some background. A need was seen among three denominations for increased involvement of youth in the ministries of their churches in Georgia. These denominations, the Christian Church (Disciples of Christ), the Episcopal Church and the United Church of Christ, under the sponsorship and auspices of Joint Educational Development looked at the

19

needs in the area, assessed the resources available to them and determined the overarching goals for this youth ministry project. They decided that the best way to meet the need for enhancing the participation of youth in their churches was to call together a team of young adults who would work intensely for a period of fifteen months to realize these goals.

The team consisted of three young adults between the ages of sixteen and twenty-two, who worked full time in three specific target areas of Georgia. The team was integrated and worked in churches with both black and white members, concentrating on those smaller congregations in the rural parts of the target areas. The project statement gave the overall purpose as "increasing levels of youth participation in congregations and judicatories (of participating denominations) and in their policy-making and program-forming structures".

The specific goals developed by an on-site team of youth and adults, were that by the end of the fifteen months:

- Youth in the participating denominations in the target areas will compose 10–20% of the policy-forming and decision-making structures in the judicatory and participating local congregations.
- Fifty per cent of the congregations in the participating denominations will have had youth reached by the Georgia Youth Empowerment Team.
- Ten per cent of the participating congregations will be involved in identifiable action groups developed around issues involving youth.
- There will be at least one statewide ecumenical youth event.

These three young adults were given housing, food and transportation plus a small living stipend for the time they were part of the GYET. Their training in youth ministry and leadership skills, communication, and group process were given by staff from the national headquarters of the three denominations and a local staff supervisor who worked with them throughout the project. The staff plus a core group of volunteer youth and adults from each of the target areas were part of an advisory and support group dubbed "the Macon Bunch", so called because they met in Macon, Georgia, a central location. The Macon Bunch offered continuing support and resources to the team as they worked. Volunteer members of the Macon Bunch managed the project budget. The entire Bunch served as periodic evaluators of the Team's operations, observing overall how they were meeting goals and objectives, and specifically how they worked with local churches. Support groups were also set up in each of the three target areas to facilitate contact with congregations in that area and to secure housing for the team members while they traveled in that area. These support groups were valuable in helping to communicate the needs and happenings of youth ministry in that area to the GYET.

The objectives for youth empowerment in these areas were not only to give those youth who participated an understanding of what they could contribute to the churches, but also to give them skills with which to be active leaders. Through a variety of exercises and discussions, these youth learned and then demonstrated skills in planning, program development, problem solving, issue action/reflection and faith exploration. They also developed the ability to empower these leadership skills in other youth. Empowerment also happened through sharing among those youth who were involved in these programs. Those young people who were already more actively involved in their local churches offered encouragement and insights to the less active youth.

Through leading a series of overnight and weekend planning and training retreats in each target area, the team was able to give the young people who participated a deeper understanding of their faith, insights into the ministry styles of their local youth groups and program planning and implementation skills. These youth also learned about the polity of their de-

21

nominations and how to participate more fully in the whole life of their churches.

These retreats formed a progression designed to help the young people learn and then test their skills. In a series of six events, they progressed from having the time planned and led by the team to planning and leading it themselves.

In addition to these events, the GYET traveled to several local churches, working with the young people of that church in faith explorations, planning skills, communications and group building exercises. These types of learning experiences were also used by the team in several summer camp settings.

Developing action groups around issues that involved youth was another area where the team gave time and energy. As a result, several congregations in the target areas organized awareness/action workshops on lifestyles, sexuality, unemployment, career development, and assertiveness training.

This is only a capsule sketch of the fifteen-month ministry of the Georgia Youth Empowerment Team. It obviously contained much more work and activity than there is space to give here. Some of the learnings that were gathered from this project, however, are valuable to share here in more length.

One recognition was that a project like this requires more than fifteen months to complete the goals and objectives adequately. Two-to-three years seemed to be a more realistic time frame. It was also realized that a firmly established communication network and already organized denominational structure are needed from the very beginning to promote an effective ministry, or at least, time designated for that process prior to the launching of the youth empowerment team.

The most significant learnings involved those gained by working with young people directly. Some of these were:

• Youth learned to become more responsible and reliable when encouraged to be so.

- Youth ministering to youth was a dynamic and successful model.
- Youth were effective leaders among their peers.
- If youth were involved in planning and decision-making processes, they had a higher investment in the program, assumed more responsibility and participated more fully.
- Community building was instrumental in enabling people to work together more effectively.
- It was important that youth leaders were trained in group process skills so that they could identify people's needs, could encourage them to be open to new ideas and understand what hinders growth.
- Youth do want to get involved in church structures.
- The modeling of women in leadership roles was important and well received.
- Both youth and adults would go to great lengths to participate in a program in which they believed.
- An integrated team was a challenging and effective model.
- Ecumenical involvement broadened the experience of both youth and adults.
- Open, challenging, trusting, accepting, respectful, deepening relationships were important for enabling personal and programmatic growth and for coping with issues.

These learnings from the GYET were significant and important because they gave tried and true evidence that youth empowerment was possible. Their initial assertions had said that youth, given responsibility, support and an opportunity for involvement in church activities, could be worthy and valuable assets to the church in all areas of its ministry. Their experiences proved this. As team member Carol Blakely pointed out in her article, it was a revolutionary thought, and a realizable one. Over and over, the experiences of GYET affirmed that youth empowerment—youth as leaders, youth as decision-makers, youth reaching out and ministering to adults and peers—was an exciting and viable form of youth ministry. In local churches such as the historic church in Midway, Georgia, youth were now represented on all the decision-making committees in the church. On the judicatory level youth were elected from their churches to be delegates to the annual conference meeting of the Southeast Conference (of which Georgia is a part). Youth were also involved in planning some parts of the meeting. One young person was elected from the Conference to be a delegate to the bienniel denominational General Synod. And as a final support, the Conference budget was rearranged to give continuing support to an offshoot of the GYET, the Southeast Conference Youth Core.

In Georgia, youth empowerment was a reality. The work and beliefs of those many people were beginning to make a difference.

CHAPTER THREE

Variations
on the Theme

Youth empowerment can work for you. Or more accurately, youth empowerment can bring a new awareness and an added dimension to the life of the church in which you are involved, and the youth ministry in which you are active.

Though many of our examples describe activities which have happened in clusters of churches and teams which have operated on the judicatory level, youth empowerment is possible in other configurations. Concepts, theories and programs which have been used in judicatories can be adapted for use in the local church and vice versa.As has been said before, you can apply these concepts to the youth ministry of which you are a part. You need to decide which styles of youth ministry are right for you and your situation.

Begin this process by looking briefly at the local church or judicatory where you are involved. Is youth empowerment at work there? Where are all the young people? In what ways are they involved in the life of your congregation or judicatory? Is there a youth voice on committees and commissions? Try this short exercise.

Journal Jottings VI:

Down the left side of a sheet of paper space out these seven categories:

• Education
• Mission/Social Issues
• Evangelism/Outreach
• Worship
• Stewardship
• Maintenance/General
• Other

These are seven areas of the work of the church. In each denomination through each local church these areas of ministry are carried out by different committees, task groups, fellowships, boards and individuals.

Beside each of these areas on your sheet, list the specific titles of those groups or individuals who have responsibilities for this area in your local church or in your judicatory. For example:

Worship: Pastor, Altar Guild, Youth Group (one service per year), Lay Speakers, Diaconate

Maintenance/General: Building Committee, Janitor, Church Secretary, Board of Trustees

Mission/Social Issues: World Hunger Study Group, Refugee Placement Task Force, Fair Housing Committee, Nuclear Disarmament Task Force

Education: Board of Christian Education, Bible Study Group, Pastor, Youth Group, Curriculum Development Committee, Church School Program, Director of Christian Education, Church School Superintendent

Try to place as many of the specific groups and special individuals that you can think of who are part of the ministry of your church.

26

Now go through your entire sheet and place a check beside those groups where young people are full participants. Take your time. Try and be as accurate as you can. If you don't have the information, do some investigation. Contact the chairperson/president of your church board or your pastor. Ask your judicatory staff consultant or area minister. They may be able to give you more information.

What do your results tell you? How involved are young people in your church or judicatory? Are they more active in some areas than others? How do *you* feel about the status of youth involvement in your church? Share some of your findings and feelings with someone else in your church family. Discuss together what you would like to see happening with young people in your church's or judicatory's ministry.

Often it is helpful as you are looking at your own situation to hear how other groups have focused on their needs and developed programs to meet those needs. The following vignettes describe various needs that different denominations have found in their youth ministries, and the responses they have initiated to meet those needs. As you read through some of these models in youth empowerment, reflect on similarities and differences with your own ministry.

Episcopal Church: Dayton Region, Diocese of Southern Ohio Youth Empowerment Team.

Though it was known that there were many leaders among the youth in the parishes of the Dayton Region and that there were some creative ministries happening in local congregations, in general these were isolated and unknown to each other. There was a need for greater participation by committed young people in the leadership of youth ministry on the regional level. Youth activities which were happening in the region and on the diocesan and provincial levels as well were unknown to most young people. And in some congregations there were such a small number of youth that the need to get together in a peer group within the church could be met only with regional or cluster activities. Thus it was felt that there was a need to bring together a cadre of persons—youth from the parishes along with a part-time coordinator—to be active and visible forces in the planning, execution and support of youth ministry in the Dayton Region.

It was decided to sponsor a Youth Empowerment Team composed of high school youth in the Dayton area. A team of three to six youth between the ages of fourteen and eighteen was sought, who had a commitment to Jesus Christ and were active within their local parish. The purpose of the team was to provide leadership training, and resources and ideas to congregations who wanted to revitalize their youth ministries. The team was also to design and give leadership to youth events involving the sixteen churches in the region, to actively promote participation in diocesan and provincial youth activities, and to develop and maintain a regional communication network among young people and adult supporters. Team members were asked to participate in some facet of the work at least twice each month during the two years that the project would last. They were supervised by a part-time youth coordinator, a young adult active in regional youth work.

Training in program planning, communication skills, group process, community building and evaluation as well as faith exploration and orientation to the Episcopal Church structure was given during the first two months.

During the term of the project, the team found that turnover in team membership was one major hurdle. Several new members were acquired as others left. Training these new members was a continual concern. In evaluation it was found that a more workable way of training would have been to conduct learning sessions initially and then again later as the need arose for expanded skills. The latter was based around specific areas of work the team was called on to do. This style would have been more valuable for skill building and more practical as new team members were added. Evaluation also affirmed that though structured learning sessions were helpful, on the job experience was the best trainer, and that reflecting on each event, both before and after, promoted the best understanding and growth.

The team goal for a regional communication network was met in part. All sixteen churches were contacted initially, and a type of telephone network was set up for the adult leaders in each parish. Though no phone network was possible for the youth, a mailing list of all young people who were active in regional events was developed. This was used to inform area youth on upcoming events and was found to increase participation of youth in sponsored activities.

The team initiated both fall and spring events for the entire region. They did the planning as well as the leadership. Their skills in group process and leadership elements were found to be the most helpful in carrying these out. The team also worked with several local churches in planning and group building for their youth groups. They were also active in recruitment for the summer camps and conferences program.

Evaluations of the project gave a very positive response to the leadership of youth by youth. Young people who were trained and experienced in skills for developing program and working with groups were able to initiate excitement and involvement among youth in the local churches. And it was also seen that local churches responded enthusiastically to the offer of individualized help in strengthening their youth ministry programming.

The regional events for senior highs were also well received. In addition, a need was expressed to expand these events and in the future programming to include events for adults working with youth to learn leadership skills and also to sponsor events for junior highs.

As a result of the Southern Ohio Youth Empowerment Team, youth ministry as a priority in the churches in the Dayton Region was highlighted; and the skills and capabilities of young people in leadership roles were seen and affirmed. The awareness of activities available within the larger church was broadened for those youth who were a part of the team and for those young people touched by the team, and youth involvement in these activities was greatly increased.

Moravian Church in North America: Youth Empowerment Team

The initial plan for the Moravian Church in North America was to set up a Youth Empowerment Team consisting of five youth plus one adult advisor in each of the six regions across Canada and the United States. A basic tenet for the formation of the teams was the realization and understanding that youth communicate best with youth, and that training a select group of young people in youth ministry skills would help them to reach out to other youth. This, in turn, would help all these young people develop a stronger personal faith and become more involved in their churches, their youth groups and their communities.

During the first year only two of the proposed teams were actually organized, one in Canada and one in the Southern region. The goals of these teams were to:

- Enhance youth ministry in the local congregations.
- Provide significant leadership training for the team members.
- Enable team members to provide peer leadership training.
- Focus the attention of the church on the need for greater youth involvement in the total life of the church.

Team members were chosen to reflect the make-up of the youth groups in the churches they would visit. In the Canadian area where most churches were small, and the youth ministry in the local church was one unified program for young people from junior high to college age, it was decided that the team would reflect this age range in its make-up: one junior high, two senior highs, one first year university student, and one person three years out of high school were chosen. The variety of ages in this team proved to be one of its strong points because they were able to relate to most levels of young people in the churches they served.

Local church empowerment was a major focus of these teams. The team from the Southern Region was active in eighteen local churches (several more than once) in helping with goal setting, programming, and other leadership and resourcing needs. They also planned and led a province-wide youth ministry workshop and a senior high weekend at an area retreat center.

Valuable learnings were gained from these two teams during the first year. At the Youth Convo of the Moravian Church the following year, so much enthusiasm and excitement about the YET concept was evidenced that the youth attending the event donated and pledged all the funds necessary to facilitate a continent-wide Youth Empowerment Team training event the following summer.

The hoped-for six teams from the six provinces plus three people participating from Labrador gathered at Laurel Ridge in North Carolina for this five day training event that next summer. Each team consisted of high school youth plus an adult advisor. The event was designed around peer training for youth ministry. Content dealt with group dynamics, leadership techniques, goal setting and learning about the structures, doctrine, history and tradition of the Moravian Church.

Recognizing the importance of enabling a collected group of

people from across each regional area to begin to feel and function like a team, a great amount of time was spent in group building and in developing a team ownership of and commitment to the goals of the project. The major goal of strengthening youth ministry in local churches was broken into these objectives:

- To communicate with youth.
- To encourage effective youth participation in the local congregation.
- To share new models/alternatives for youth ministry.
- To aid in the evaluation of a local congregation's youth ministry.
- To facilitate youth/adult dialogues on youth needs, youth involvement in the church and the role of adults working with youth.
- To educate youth concerning the structure and the functioning of the church as an institution and the possible roles (positions) they could serve.

Teams also spent considerable time developing specific strategies to accomplish these objectives in their own regional areas. These would be done in some regions through area seminars and workshops, in others through team visits to local churches.

One highlight of this total project was the high degree of enthusiasm and commitment that was felt and shown by those young people who were members of the teams, and the growth in Christian commitment that was evidenced. This can probably best be summed up in one team's motto:

"To teach . . . yet still learn.
To lead . . . yet still serve.
To share . . . yet still listen.
To act . . . yet still pray."

United Church of Christ: Southeast Conference
Youth Core

As a result of the work of the Georgia Youth Empowerment Team, several churches in Georgia received help and input into their youth ministry programs. The excitement and enthusiasm which resulted from these churches, both for their own programming and for getting together with other churches, led the conference programming board and the denominational national staff to look toward future planning after the conclusion of the GYET projects.

A core group of active and interested young people from churches with both Black and white membership in Georgia had been built up through involvement with the GYET. However, there were still many churches in Georgia and other areas of the Southeast Conference, which also includes Alabama and Tennessee, in need of stimulation in their youth ministry programming. Many of these were small rural churches separated by great distances from other United Church of Christ churches. Only a few had participated in youth activities beyond their local church and several had no youth program at all.

Building on the enthusiasm of this core group and the interest and willingness of the United Church Board for Homeland Ministries, a national agency, to fund and train projects for integrated and empowered youth for ministry, the Southeast Conference initiated the Youth Core.

The overall purpose of the Youth Core was to strengthen youth ministry programming within the churches of the Southeast Conference. A planning group of eight youth and adults from the Youth Core met for a day-long planning conference. One major decision from that planning session was to hold a series of three weekend retreats. Youth and adults of the Youth Core would come to all three retreats and be trained in leadership skills, faith development skills, communication techniques, group building, goal setting, program planning and implementation. These youth and adults would then use these skills in their own churches and would also be available to resource other local churches in their area.

Twenty-four youth and six adults, black and white, urban and rural, gathered monthly over a three month period for the series of leadership retreats. Response was positive and the creative talents and capabilities shown by the young people were exceptional.

During the first year the skills gained at the leadership weekends were put to use mainly in the local churches of the participants. The outreach to other area churches was minimal. Many churches were somewhat skeptical of this new project of youth's being leaders. Also there was a lack of continuity in the adult leadership coordinating the project within the conference. No one adult volunteer could devote the time needed to promote and support the Youth Core as was necessary.

At the start of the second year, a part-time Youth Core Coordinator was hired to help support and spread the talents and skills of the Youth Core to other churches. Again three leadership retreat weekends were held, with many of the original young people returning. With the time, effort, and support of the Coordinator, the Youth Core was able to use skills gained at the weekends in helping several other local churches in their youth ministry programming. They also led cluster events for churches in their areas and were active at the Annual Conference Meeting, taking several leadership roles.

The concept and creation of the Youth Core was an effective new idea to the churches in the Southeast Conference. The first year was somewhat of a breaking-in period. Openness to and excitement for the idea and encouragement for churches getting involved with the Youth Core were much stronger the second year. News of some tested accomplishments in certain local churches the first year spread, and enthusiasm across the Conference grew.

Having a strong support group of concerned adults also proved to be one of the key factors in the strength of the Youth Core. Those young people who were supported by adults, lay and clergy, in their own local church were much stronger contributors to the youth ministry programming in their own church and in the resourcing of other churches in their area. The presence during the second year of the Youth Core Coordinator demonstrated this also. Having the institutional support through the Coordinator was a vital element in the young people's outreach to other area churches, both in making the contacts and in being a resource to them in planning for cluster events or local church programming.

The integrated nature of the group was also an important asset. It promoted the acceptance of the Youth Core by the conference churches as a valid and realistic form of ministry for their area.

Most importantly, the Southeast Conference Youth Core revived a spirit of excitement about youth ministry within the conference. It started a snowballing effect among many of the churches by raising an awareness that young people are ready, willing and able to be active participants in their churches and to share their skills in ministry with others.

Several common threads run through all these stories. The main one tells us that youth reaching out to youth, sharing their faith, enabling their leadership, resourcing their needs, and supporting their struggles is a valuable form of ministry. This is youth empowerment. It works. Youth are capable of being leaders and of teaching their skills to other youth and to adults.

Another common thread reinforces the idea that a high level of commitment and enthusiasm must exist among the young people who are part of a youth empowerment model if there is going to be a significant outreach. The young people involved must feel a commitment to the goals of the project and an enthusiasm and confidence for reaching out to others to share their skills. This commitment is gained when the benefits and value of their efforts are continually visible and reinforced. It is heightened if the youth feel the strong and continuous support of adults working with them. Adults who care and are available as resources to the young people are an essential catalyst to a youth empowerment effort.

Though the turnover rate for high school participants can be high, it is lowered if the commitment level of the young people and the adults is stronger. The planners of a project, however, need to be aware of turnover and plan for it as they train and build their teams. Inclusion of new and old members should be a constant process.

One final significant dynamic was that these young people felt good about sharing their faith with others. Growth in their faith in Jesus Christ and in their relationships with other Christians was highlighted on nearly every evaluation of both youth and adults in all models. "The Youth Empowerment Team has been a rewarding Christian growth experience for me," said Beth Shouse of one Moravian YET. "Disappointment has been mixed with joy and I felt this was Christ's way of telling me that life has its ups and downs, but not to give up for He will not forsake His own.[1]

Ministering to and with each other is what we are called to do as Christians. And enabling young people in the skills and understanding for *ministering to* and *with each other* is what we're called to do in youth empowerment. Believing in youth empowerment is believing that this ministry of young people needs to be an essential part as the Christian community strives for wholeness.

Note

1. Sutherland, ibid., p. 7.

Part II

Youth Empowerment— How?

CHAPTER FOUR

Planning for Youth Empowerment

Youth empowerment has proven to be a valuable form of ministry in many judicatories. These judicatories have had rewarding results in strengthening the youth ministry of the regional levels and in empowering the ministry of local churches that have participated. New programs have been initiated, new enthusiasm inspired and the involvement of young people increased significantly in the areas of those churches where youth have assumed an active part in the planning and leadership.

Youth empowerment can work. And it can work in your own situation. Planning is essential. Planning begins with a close examination of who you are, what you have to work with, what you need to be doing and where you want to be going. It should involve all the young people and adults who will be active in the program leadership.

Youth empowerment is built around recognizing the needs of youth and ministering to and with them, and involving and enabling them to help each other meet those needs. It is facilitating their empowerment in the planning and leadership of their own special ministry and in the ministry of the whole church at work. It is young people and adults supporting each other as they live out this ministry.

Planning is the framework for establishing your own youth empowerment model. Viable and enriching youth ministry programs do not just happen. They require much research, development and action. The youth empowerment planning process begins by reflecting on the Christian commitment which brings you together. It moves on to look at the people who make up your ministry and those who will be active in your youth empowerment efforts. It includes the development of goals and objectives. It continues through to the evaluating of what you have accomplished, identifying what you have learned and what that means to you. Its conclusion (and commencement) celebrates a job well done (or just done) and the worshipful thanks for the presence of God's guidance and support throughout, with renewed commitment for the next phase.

Why such an extensive planning process? Because it is important for people involved to know each other and feel comfortable with one another before needs, concerns and challenges can be shared effectively and a team can be built. It is important that all involved be part of the leadership and implementation and use the talents and skills which each has to contribute. It is important that evaluation and reflection be a continual dynamic so that growth is intentional and deliberate.

The importance of thorough planning can be illustrated by a comparison of good planning with successful firebuilding. An amateur might say that to light a match to whatever arrangement of wood and scraps is an adequate means for enkindling a roaring, enduring blaze. The experienced camper or firebuilder knows that there are certain types of wood, different sizes and proper stacking needed to produce a healthy fire. Our amateur will, of course, succeed sometimes; but more often than not, the paper, small chips, and dried leaves will burn out quickly and the fire will die away. The big logs will never ignite to keep the blaze burning till the embers glow. So it is with some youth ministry efforts. Some social events or special trips will spark a blaze of interest for their short duration, but the continuing involvement and support are not there.

With proper firebuilding you begin with the smallest twigs and stack on larger kindling, working up to the largest logs on the top. With proper planning, you look at the basic needs of the people and the challenges of the faith, and then build and expand your ministry from these. Each piece of wood ignites with those around it and then with those above it to create a final steady blaze. Each person contributes those skills and talents which are unique to him or her. These talents complement each other and as leadership and resources are shared, new skills are learned. Persons enable and challenge one another as they work together. This support system helps make the blaze of interest constant and, like the smoldering embers, is used to spark another flame.

Basic Questions for Planning

The simple question of who, what, when, where and how are valuable ones to ask at any stage of planning. As you begin the planning process for your own youth empowerment team, it is valuable to respond to these questions as you set the context for planning. Look at each separately and answer it in relation to how your group will work through the actual planning process session by session.

The first question is "who". Who should be involved? To promote full ownership in the outcomes, it is always best to include in the planning process all who are active in or have decision-making power about youth ministry program and

41

budget. Only in this way can the wide range of interest and potential be taken into consideration. Some questions to consider as you look at the people to be involved in the process are: Who are those young people who are involved or have potential to be involved in the team and the programming? Who are the adults who provide support to and advocacy for youth in the church? Who are other leaders within the church or community who could be valuable resources to your planning? Who will be affected by your ministry? What church staff or committee member would be helpful? What areas of the work of the church do you want to look at or need to know more about? You may think of other questions which can help you focus on those who would be valuable participants and contributors.

The "how" is the method by which you will work toward the goal. The "what" is the ballpark goal that you hope to accomplish. You may say that for you this goal is building an effective youth team in your church or judicatory. In this case it would be through the use of a planning process incorporating the concepts of youth empowerment, measurable objectives, the actual implementation of the strategies and evaluation, and reflection.

The answers to the "when" and "where" are more situational. They are dependent on your group and the resources available to you. The "where" refers to the place in which you will hold the sessions as you go through the planning process. This can be anywhere: church basement, youth room, home(s) of participants, or retreat center—any place that is large enough to hold comfortably everyone who is involved and has the wall space to post all the sheets of ideas that your group will generate. Tables and chairs are helpful at various points, but random seating in a circle in comfortable chairs or on the floor can be most conducive to open discussion and idea sharing. A more comfortable, cheerful, and appealing physical atmosphere always enriches any planning session

Though not absolutely necessary, it may also be helpful to have extra rooms for small group meetings, recreational activities and snack areas. You can determine what setting(s) will be most appropriate for your group.

The "when" query is the time that you want to hold the planning sessions and the length you want them to be. This is determined by the planning design you use. More participants and cooperation from the people involved usually results if you first determine the amount of time that they are willing to commit. A planning group may find their plan thwarted if they have chosen a design where the sessions extend over three weekends and their group is only willing to commit one weekend or possibly two or three long afternoon sessions at Sunday meetings.

The undergirding word is not a question—it is a necessary, unequivocal, essential commitment. As much as possible, those who agree to participate should commit themselves for the total time allotted for the planning process. Occasional participation hinders understanding of how the process works and how the results have come about. It limits ownership in these results. It is also unfair to the others who contribute their time and energy throughout. From previous models we can see how ownership in the program is strongly related to a person's future participation, contribution and the personal value they receive from it. So, when you discuss the planning process and consequently the time commitment involved, the benefits to both the total outcome of your ministry and to each individual person should be stressed. Some groups find that a written covenant signed beforehand works best to explain and to insure commitment. Others find that an open discussion and verbal covenants have been worthwhile. Continual reinforcement of each person's value and contributions to the teamwork throughout each step in the planning also helps strengthen commitment.

Open communication enhances commitment. Because of

this, repeated discussion about why you are planning is essential. Begin at the onset with explanations on the theories and dynamics of youth empowerment. Explore the feelings and ideas of those participating. You might use some of the journal exercises you have done earlier on youth ministry and the church. Help others develop their own definition of youth ministry through looking at the challenge of the scriptures; the call to the church to work in the world; and the needs, interests and concerns of all those who participate in your youth ministry program. Review of the steps in the planning process—what will happen, and what the rewards will be—is important in helping people to experience partnership and to commit themselves to the planning and its implementation. By communicating with all those involved and affirming the need for their time, ideas and talents for the success of youth ministry efforts, you incorporate an essential dynamic of empowerment calling persons forth toward their best potential.

Ten Steps in Planning

There are ten steps in this planning process. Each is important and builds on the one before it. The time needed for each step varies and often depends on the creativity and needs of your group. This list is an outline of the steps with a capsule description. Following this outline, each step is further explained with ideas and exercises for doing it.

Step 1: Theological reflection—
   Acknowledge, celebrate, deepen and strengthen our commitment within the Christian community.
Step 2: Build a Community of Love, Mutuality, Respect, and Power—
Get to know the people in your group; develop an open atmosphere for sharing, challenging and caring.

44

Step 3: Articulating a Reason for Being—
Develop a purpose/mission statement for the group: the description of intent for the work of the team.

Step 4: Setting Goals—
Find out the needs, interests and concerns the members intend to address. Set targets for meeting their needs in a general period of time.

Step 5: Stating Objectives—
Outline specific, measurable intentions which guide the team in meeting their overarching goal.

Step 6: Brainstorming Strategies—
List the detailed steps which lead to the fulfillment of each objective.

Step 7: Setting a Timetable—
Chart all the specifics of the strategies; set a date for the accomplishment of each specific task and leadership responsibilities for each.

Step 8: Actions, Programs, and Projects—
Do it.

Step 9: Evaluation—
Assess, through either written or oral form, the learnings from the experience or action; identify strengths, weaknesses. Review styles of action as well as the specific action for consistency in meeting the goal and statement of purpose of the team.

Step 10: Celebration—
Celebrate growth, accomplishments and learnings; express gratitude to God and to those who were a part of your ministry; Affirm the gifts contributed by the team to accomplish the objectives achieved.

Step 1: Theological Reflection

Each gathering of your group should include a celebration of the Christian bond and love which bring us together, and the challenge to which our Christian faith calls us. The period for theological reflection should be included where it fits most appropriately for your group. It is included here first because of the primary role it has in the whole concept of youth empowerment.

Theological reflection is thinking about the "God connection." It is essential to youth ministry. Without it, youth ministry would be an exercise in humanitarian growth or psychological development. These are both valuable and commendedable concerns but youth ministry's distinction is in its religious grounding. What makes youth ministry unique is that its center is Jesus Christ, and its expression is in a community of faith, the church.

Theological reflection in and about youth ministry is the act of exploring the biblical and traditional understandings of Jesus Christ and the nature and mission of the church today. Youth ministry should be examined in relationship to the whole of ministry. Theological reflection provides the grounding for our work and a plumb line for the evaluation of our lives and the work of the church.

The following three readings and exercises provide a beginning for this task. There are many ways it might be done. The important point is that it be done, remembering that there is "yet more light to break forth from the word of God."

The Risk of Discipleship

Read aloud: Luke 9:57–62.
Allow some time for silent or group response.
Then read:

It is not difficult to make beautiful, generous statements in the excitement and ecstasy of some new commitment.

The expressions of gratitude and the pledges of love an loyalty that result from some revelation of or insight into God's redeeming love are precious indeed.

46

They are, nonetheless, often shallow and immature.

There are so many who accept Christ as Savior and Redeemer and verbally, at least, honor Him as Lord, who never mature into disciples.

Apart from being personally solaced and comforted, the lives of these people never change very much.

They have never really become Christ's disciples and servants.

They are obviously not ready or willing to pay the price involved in the matter of discipleship.

Of course there is a price to pay—or so it seems to you who have never, as Christ did, beheld the glories of God's kingdom.

Because you have not seen nor can possibly comprehend the full meaning of your redemption and the life that awaits you, the things of this world, though they are trinkets when compared to what is in store for you, are still very important.

Discipleship involves a risk—or so it will appear in your eyes.

Jesus can at this time only assure you that it is a risk worth taking.

You have nothing to lose and everything to gain in following after Him.

If you really believe in Him you will, inspired and encouraged by the Holy Spirit, fling caution to the winds and dare to trust in His words and to obey His commandments.

He does not guarantee perpetual happiness or ecstatic feelings.

He promises, instead, that there will be conflict and pain, heavy burdens and difficult times.

He promises as well, Jesus does, that you will never be alone—that He is with you always and will grant you His joy.[1]

Every Christian a Servant

Read aloud: Matthew 23:1–12
Allow some time for silent or group response.
Then read:

If you are delegated leadership as a result of your aspiring or striving, it is a precarious position that you assume.

Those who are truly led by the Spirit of God into positions of leadership will often be considered to be "losers" by the world-at-large.

This is because they follow Jesus Christ, and His leadership is synonymous with servanthood.

It is because they, rather than resolving the conflicts and problems of this world, point to the new kingdom and to their God, who alone can resolve the conflicts and struggles of humanity.

Rather than promoting themselves and their own glory, they lead people in glorifying God.

Instead of promising people success, they challenge them to make sacrifices; instead of comforting them in their self-centeredness and apathy, they provoke them into accepting responsibility for the poor and less fortunate about them.

Instead of being the leaders of people, they take the lead in being servants to people—seeking to lead them into spiritual fulfillment, as well as responding to their physical needs.

This is because they are lovers of people rather than masters of people, and they dedicate themselves to communicating, in word and deed, God's saving love and grace to His Creatures about them.

In this manner and measure you are all called to be leaders and teachers, servants of your heavenly Father.[2]

A Theological Framework

In Ginny Holderness' book, *Youth Ministry,* is a very helpful and challenging statement, "Youth Ministry: A Theological Frame of Reference." This statement could be shared with the group, allowing time for silent reading, underlining the three most important passages and then sharing with one another the value of Holderness' statement as it affects the lives of individuals and the team.

Another way of approaching this theological framework is by having the group list the most meaningful words for them under each of these categories:

CHURCH   FAITH   FAITHFULNESS   MINISTRY   YOUTH MINISTRY

Then have participants form sentences using words from three or more of the columns. The point is to make connections among the categories. These statements can then either stand on their own or be the basis for the group's "Theological Frame of Reference". Introduce Holderness' statement when it would be affirming and/or complementary to the process.

Youth Ministry: A Theological Frame of Reference

Youth ministry cannot exist apart from the church.

The goal of youth ministry is the same as that of the church—that all members be involved in the total life of the congregation, which includes its worship, study, congregational ministry, service, and fellowship.

Youth are members of the community of faith, the church, now. They are not future members.

The church is founded on Jesus Christ and is commissioned to proclaim God's goodness, power, and love.

The purpose of the church is to take up the difficult and glorious struggle of knowing and doing the will of God. Youth are involved in this struggle.

49

The community of faith is the teacher of the young. Youth learn about the Christian faith by participating in the life of the church, not just by the church school.

The community of faith is a community of change and challenge. The challenge for the church today is to participate in the transformation of the world on behalf of the good news of Jesus Christ.

Youth ministry is necessary so that the church can:

—respond to the specific needs of youth;

—support its young people;

—offer a context and a place in which youth can get together with their peers;

—offer youth opportunities to explore, question, and grow through various stages of commitment.[3]

Our values and style of life should be a result of our faithful response to Jesus Christ.[4]

Being faithful means searching for ways to respond as the community of faith to the issues in our everyday lives and in a changing society. The challenge for the church today is to participate in the transformation of the world on the basis of the good news of Jesus Christ. This means that as a church we—children, youth, and adults—continually seek to bring good news to the poor, liberation to the oppressed, and justice and peace to all persons.[5]

Step 2: Group Building

The establishment of a community of caring and challenge within your group is the most important element of your planning. Developing a circle of belonging where one feels comfortable, free to share thoughts and feelings, secure in being challenged to grow and respond, and safe enough to ask questions and voice concerns or fear, is one of the important goals for the youth empowerment team and for those with whom the youth minister.

We gather together as a church to support and affirm our Christianity and to work and grow together as we live out our faith. This happens most meaningfully within a group where we are affirmed as an important contributing person.

Group building exercises provide one process for nurturing community within both the youth team and among the people with whom the team interacts. Group building exercises may be categorized as follows:

- *Getting Acquainted*—telling others your name, then giving some factual information about yourself: height, hair color, favorite food, types of music you enjoy or where you live.
- *Sharing Yourself*—giving more details about yourself, such as, your favorite time of day, what makes you angry, special moments you have had or experiences from your childhood. These exercises include affirming others as they share themselves with you.
- *Revealing Feelings*—giving more in-depth thoughts, feelings and personal history about who you are as a person and as a Christian; risking and sharing the more personal concerns about yourself, your needs, your fears, your faith and your future. These exercises also include giving feedback and support to other people in the group and establishing an atmosphere of love, challenge and acceptance.

Following are some samples of exercises that might be used in each of the categories:

Getting Acquainted

Wiggam

Everyone should sit in a circle. The leader picks up a random object (the larger and more unusual the better) and christens it the "Wiggam". Holding the Wiggam, she says, "This is a Wiggam. I am passing this Wiggam from Terri (her name) to you." She then hands the Wiggam to the person on her right, Tod. Tod then turns to the person on his right and says, "This is a Wiggam. And I am passing this Wiggam from Terri to Tod to _____." This continues around the entire circle with each succeeding person repeating all the names that come prior to him or her. The last person will be naming all the people in the circle. This works best for groups numbering between ten to twenty.[6]

Variation: Each person tacks a hobby they may have on to the end of their name. Thus, the first person may become Terri Drawing and the second Tod Photography and so on. People must remember both names and hobbies as they pass the Wiggam.

Find the Person Who. . . .

Circulate among the people in the room and get the signature of any person who answers the description of any of the statements. You must approach each new person and ask them about a specific statement (until you find one which fits them); for example, "Are you wearing striped socks?" No person can sign your sheet twice. Find the person who:

1. Plays the piano._____
2. Is wearing striped socks._____
3. Traveled the farthest to get here._____
4. Plays the guitar._____
5. Was the first to arrive._____
6. Read their Bible today._____
7. Helps in Sunday School._____
8. Was not born in Ohio._____
9. Whose grandparents live in Florida._____
10. Has been to a youth rally before._____
11. Likes lemon pie._____
12. Is in the band._____
13. Is a vegetarian._____
14. Helped in a political campaign._____

15. Likes classical music._____
16. Plays the clarinet._____
17. Sings in the church choir._____
18. Plays the tuba._____
19. Has the longest name._____
20. Attended the denomination's annual (biennial) meeting._____
21. Likes rock n' roll music._____
22. Went to church camp last summer._____
23. Has attached ear lobes._____
24. Is a hiking and/or camping enthusiast._____
25. Can locate the carburetor under the hood of a car.___

Stacked Seats

Form chairs into a circle. Each person must have a chair, but have no extras. The statements listed below should be read one at a time: Those people having a positive response to the statement should move the indicated number of chairs to the right or left. If there is already a person sitting in the chair someone else is approaching, he/she must sit on the other's lap. Occasionally more than two or three people end up on the same chair. The object is for one person to make one complete trip around the circle to the right and pass the chair where they originally started. Some possible statements for the leader to read aloud:

1. If your mother wears tennis shoes, move two chairs to the right.
2. If you are wearing anything brown, move one chair to the right.
3. If you have blond hair, move three chairs to the right.
4. If you have green eyes, move two chairs to the right.
5. If you wear glasses, move one chair to the left.
6. If you are wearing a watch, move two chairs to the right.
7. If you are wearing tennis shoes, move one chair to the right.

8. If you read the Bible today, move five chairs to the right.
9. If you have a person on your lap, move. . . .
10. If you are sixteen or under, move. . . .
11. If you like liver, move. . . .
12. If you know who Ronald Reagan is, move. . . .
13. If you've ever been to a youth rally before, move. . . .
14. If you've ever been to a church camp, move. . . .
15. If you are a girl, move. . . .
16. If you are a boy, move. . . .
17. If your father owns a red tie, move. . . .
18. If you live in a brick house, move. . . .
19. If you serve on a committee at your church, move. . . .
20. If your family has a red car, move. . . .
21. If you play a musical instrument, move. . . .
22. If your father wears pink polka-dotted pajamas, move. . . .
23. If you are wearing white socks, move. . . .
24. If you are wearing blue jeans, move. . . .
25. If your birthday is in June, move. . . .
26. If your middle name starts with L, move. . . .
27. If you have naturally curly hair, move. . . .
28. If you do exercises at least once a week, move. . . .
29. If you own a dog, move. . . .
30. If you are on the bottom of the chair, move. . . .
31. (Think up some of your own.)

MEET ZAGGY

We've all probably met a forlorn cartoon character that seems to caricature a lot of every person's ingredients. Here's a chance for each person to share something of himself or herself in this get acquainted exercise. Draw Zaggy (or create your own version) on a board or newsprint. Give each participant a piece of newsprint about 14- by 22-inches in size and a felt-tip pen, and ask them to copy your drawing, writing or drawing in the responses as indicated. When everyone is finished have them share their drawing and responses with the rest of the group.[7]

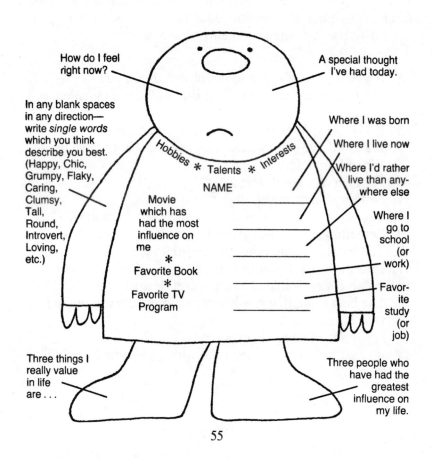

Sharing Yourself

Moving Lines

Have the entire group form two lines facing each other. Each person sits down facing a person in the opposite line. The leader will begin a statement. Each person in a pair takes time to complete the statement. When all have finished, the leader will call "Move" and each person will move one person to the right and face a new partner. Those people on the right ends of the lines will switch to the opposite line. The leader will then begin another statement. The lines rotate each time after completing a statement until the list of statements has been discussed. Some statements to use can be:

1. A person I would like to be for one day. . . .
2. If I had to get along without one modern convenience, I would give up. . . .
3. If I could splurge on something I would get. . . .
4. If I could live somewhere else, I would want to live in. . . .
5. When I am angry I. . . .
6. My idea of a good time is. . . .
7. Nothing burns me up like. . . .
8. The thing that gives me the greatest satisfaction is. . . .
9. Something that really concerns me right now is. . . .
10. The most exciting thing I ever did was. . . .
11. One word that describes me is. . . .
12. When I was a child, I had a secret desire to be. . . .
13. The best thing that has happened in my church in the last year is. . . .
14. A person I feel really close to is. . . .
15. If I could throw caution to the wind right now I would like to. . . .

All About Me

Ask each person to think about adjectives which describe themselves. On a sheet of paper have them (1) list ten to fifteen words or phrases which they feel describe them. This should include both positive and negative, physical and personality characteristics. When this is completed, ask them (2) to list five words or phrases which would describe how they think *others* see them.

Finally have each person (3) write three descriptive words or phrases which they *would like* other people to say about them.

This should all be done with as much silence as possible. When everyone is finished, have people form groups of three, preferably with others whom they do not know as well. Each person should share the words and phrases from the first section and tell why they selected them. When each is finished, move on to the second set of phrases and then the third.

Self Advertising

Give each person an eleven by fourteen inch sheet of paper. Provide in the center of the room a large supply of old magazines and newspapers, as well as scissors and glue. Ask each person to cut out pictures, words, and phrases from the newspapers and magazines which describe them in some way. Then each person should paste these in a collage form on the paper. Give the group thirty minutes to make their individual collages. After thirty minutes ask group members to hold up their collage in front of them and circulate *silently* for five minutes viewing each others' collages. Then form into groups of six or eight and have each person share their creation with the other members of their small groups. They should explain the significance of each element of the collage.

Revealing Feelings

Molding Feelings

Have the entire group sit in a circle. Using an imaginary piece of clay, the leader starts by molding this imaginary clay into a shape, object, or abstract form which tells something about himself or herself. This is done silently. No one is allowed to comment or to ask questions. When the leader is finished, the imaginary clay object is passed to the next person for shaping into his or her own object or abstract shape. Growing, shrinking, and changing are all allowed. When all members have had their chance at molding their feelings, have them explain to the group what they molded and why.

Variation: It is also possible to give each person his or her own piece of real modeling clay for them to shape and then describe to the group.

Back Panel

Each person attaches a large sheet of paper to his or her back with pins. Armed with pens and pencils, people circulate around the room writing on each person's back one positive comment about him or her and each of their contributions to the group. Encourage people to write on as many papers as possible. When finished, give participants time to read and reflect on their sheets. Have those individuals who care to, comment on their back panels.

Boxed-in Feelings

Give each participant a sheet of paper. Have them divide it into eight equal sections. In each section they are to write one phrase. The sheet would look like the following one. They should complete their sheets in silence. When everyone has finished, have them move into small groups of three with people they know least. They are then to discuss their answers and look at possible ways that the total group might minister to some of their needs.

One thing I am good at. . . .	One dream I have. . . .
Three things I like about myself. . . .	My greatest accomplishment in the last year. . . .
My greatest fear right now. . . .	One area in my life where I am hurting right now. . . .
One thing I would like to change about my life. . . .	Three things I need from this group. . . .

Wise Words

Ask people to bring in a poem, scripture passage, piece of prose or short story which has special meaning for them. Have them share it with the group. Then in groups of four discuss the feelings and ideas it stimulates for you. A prayer-poem like the one following could open up valuable discussion. Look at each stanza. What does it say to you? What responses does it evoke in you? Have you had similar thoughts or feelings? Reconvene in the total group after discussing the poem and share reactions.

Getting it All Together

O God,

I'm trying to get myself together.
But I need people to talk with so I can tell them who I think I am and what it means to me to be human, and then listen to what it means to them. It's as if sharing my humanness with others is the beginning of knowing myself.

I ache for friends I can trust.
No matter who I am or what I do, I need people who accept me.
When I share deep secrets, they never tell.
When I stray, they honestly question me.
When I'm at my worst, they bring out my best.

I hurt when others hurt.
I cannot be silent when the human dignity of another is abused—whether by oppression, poverty, hunger, injustice or disease.
I fight back by being informed enough to act responsibly, aggressively, patiently, but non-violently. Healing happens with time but also with wise action.

I worry about the world.
But I feel so helpless because it's all so big and beyond me.
Yet I sense that somehow there's more that is uniting us than separating us—if we were only big enough to see how alike we really are and how important we are to each other.

I feel close to nature.
I see a harmony in the order and beauty of the oneness between human beings and nature. As I study all living forms, I see my own life more clearly. No wonder the clean stream, the eager beaver, and the spider's web inspire me— there I meet all that is right as you meant it to be.

I like to have fun!
Not at the expense of others but out of sheer joy of work, play and celebration—whether it's raking leaves, studying, creating art, tutoring a child, playing basketball, praying, singing—if you really believe in what you're doing, it's easy to find the joy in it.

I dream a lot about what can be.
What's the future hold? What do I want to do with my life? What ought the world to be? Such visions fill me with hope that there's a chance for change for the better. But such visions also prod me about what is right—and wrong—for tomorrow, and today. Such visions, God, are your gift and my goal.

I know you're listening, God.
I feel your presence in nature, in friendships, and in times of trouble.
I want you to be there. However, I've got to admit that I don't always feel comfortable with you around, especially when I think I might be wrong.

Shalom![8]

Step 3: Developing a Statement of Purpose

The statement of purpose for a group is the description of intent for the existence of that group, its reason for being, its self-definition.

You may think that you and the members of your group already know this implicitly, and possibly you do. But when you sit down to talk about it, you may find that the reason for being and the expectations for involvement are different for each person. Some may be involved only for the social aspects, others for the travel, some for the leadership opportunities, others because they "want to do some good". Many may come to learn more about the Bible; several may want to be part of a service group; and others may want to influence the church agenda and programs.

Taking the time to discuss the many agendas of all the participants can avoid confusion, disappointment, and dropouts. A group can't be everything for everyone, but it can uncover and focus on several of the expectations of its members and develop a statement of purpose which reflects these.

A simple series of questions and discussion can bring out the ideas and intentions of members which can lead to developing a statement of purpose. These questions should focus on three main areas which contribute to your statement. These areas are:

• The needs, interests, and concerns of the individual members of the group.
• The challenge presented to all Christians in the scriptures.
• Our role in the church and as the church in the world today.

These areas are explored as you determine your definition of youth ministry. They are also important to explore as you develop the definition for your youth empowerment team and its program. One process for working through this could look like this:

Statement of Purpose Exercise

1. *5–10 minutes*
   In the total group make this statement, "I came to participate in this group because. . . ." Ask each person to complete this sentence aloud. Have one person write all the responses on newsprint and post them in the room so they are visible to everyone.

2. *15–20 minutes*
   Form into groups of four. In each small group complete and discuss this statement, "In my ideal youth empowerment team I want. . . ." Each small group should record their description of the ideal group on a piece of newsprint.

62

Allow fifteen to twenty minutes for discussion and recording. Reconvene in the total group and have each small group present the outcome of their discussion to the total group.

3. *15 minutes*
Now divide the group into two smaller groups.
a. The task of one group is to come up with a list which answers the statement, "Some needs which our group can meet in this church (or judicatory) are. . . ." Record these needs on newsprint.
b. The task of the other half of the group is to reflect on areas where the church should minister in the world-at-large. They should brainstorm responses to the statement: "Those areas where the church should be involved in the world today are. . . ." Record these on newsprint.

4. *10—15 minutes*
Reconvene the total group and have each group report back and post their list of ideas. Allow time after each report for members of the other group to respond and make contributions.

5. *20–30 minutes*
Divide again into groups of four. Give each group a passage of scripture. Some passages which challenge us to strengthen our Christian commitment are: Romans 12:1–13; 1 Corinthians 12:3–13, 22–27; James 1:18–27; and 1 Peter 3:8–17. Have each group read the assigned passage to interpret its meaning for our lives today. Groups should then discuss the following questions in relation to their passage:
• What does this passage challenge us to do as a church in the world?
• How does this passage challenge us as a youth team within the church?
Then have each group read their passage to the entire group and highlight the challenges they found in the verses.

6. *10–15 minutes*

All the information that has been placed on newsprint should be posted around the room so that it is visible to everyone. All the thoughts and feelings that are contained on these sheets should be considered as you think about a statement of purpose for your group.

Have the group review silently what is contained on the sheets. Then have people suggest elements that they feel should be included in a statement of purpose. Someone should record all those ideas suggested or circle them on the posted lists.

Finally, select a small group of three or four people who will review all the input the group has given and write a statement of purpose. Have the groups bring their statements to the next meeting for feedback and adoption by the group.

One example of a statement of purpose is that of the Southeast Conference Youth Core:

"To provide our churches with fresh input and initiative for youth ministry, to assist young people to come alive to the prospect of new and challenging opportunities for involvement in the church and its world-wide ministry, and to affirm the ecumenical thrust of Christian witness."

Step 4: Goal Setting

A goal is a desired achievement for a group. It is a working component of the statement of purpose. Goals are those topic or issue areas where a group wishes to focus its efforts during a particular period of time.

While the statement of purpose gives a group its guiding direction, goals identify more specific areas for concentration.

Goals are set by looking at groupings of interest, concerns, and needs of the youth team, the congregation and the community.

Following are some processes which might be used in setting goals.

Goal Setting Exercise

1. *15 to 20 minutes*

Draw the following diagram on a large sheet of paper. Post it where it is visible to the entire group.

	Last Year	Sept.—Jan.	Feb.—May	June—Aug.
Highs				
Lows				
Time				

Ask the group to think about the activities and projects that they have participated in during the past two years. Starting with the most recent time block, chart the activities and projects. Include any major problems that occurred. These activities should be put in either the high or low category of the time block depending on how the group felt about them, i.e. whether they enjoyed them or not. For example, a ski trip that was enjoyed by everyone in February would be put in the February–May box on the high side. A problem that occurred because of communication failure about organizing for the youth at the Annual Meeting would be put in the low box of September–January. The group should agree as much as possible on whether a project belongs in the high or low category. Those activities that were enjoyed only by part of the group should be put in the high category and marked with an asterisk. As much as possible, list by each activity what was positive about it and/or what was weak or needed more work.

An example of one team's survey looked like this:

	Last Year	Sept.—Jan.	Feb.—May	June—Aug.
Highs	Work trip to Appalachia Trip to amusement park Information Hotline Volunteer	Career speakers Sub Sandwich Sale Evening in Germany Dinner Fall Weekend Retreat Regional Youth Rally Peace Task Force Meetings* Leaf raking	Ski trip Planting garden at retirement village Bible study* Youth worship service Judicatory meeting	Water skiing party Senior High Camp* Gardening at retirement village Youth Leadership Planning and Training Camp*
Lows	Bake sale Lack of planning for the year Too much expected of adult leaders	Barbeque for church (Lack of organization and planning) Lack of communication about transportation for youth to the Annual Meeting	Rap sessions (Lack of coordination and agenda) Changing meeting plans at last minute Failed "disarmament proposal" during the church meeting	

After finishing, give the group a chance to look over the listing, especially noting what type of activities the group enjoyed and what type they didn't, and what things were enjoyed by part of the group. Examine also what problems were encountered, and what some positive learnings from these problems were.

2. *20 Minutes*

Divide into groups of four to six people Still focusing the group's attention on the chart, ask, "What does it appear that you value as a group?". This does not mean specific activities, but rather generalized statements about these

66

activities. Each small group should review the highs and lows and record on newsprint the value statements they perceive. Disliked activities can also be indicators of positive values.

The following example may be helpful to clarify the task. It is a continuation of the previous example.

"What does it appear that you value as a group?"

- Service projects that provide worthwhile help for others
  —Work camp to Appalachia, leaf raking for senior citizens, gardening at the retirement village, staffing the Information Hotline.
- Trips for fun and fellowship
  —Trip to amusement park, ski trip, water skiing party.
- Getting involved in church (local and judicatory) committees and programs
  —Youth Rally, Peace Task Force, senior high camp, Youth Leadership Planning and Training Camp, judicatory (budget; long-range planning) meeting.
- Creative money making projects
  —Sub Sandwich Sale, Evening in Germany Dinner, low rating on bake sale.
- Chances to grow in our faith
  —Bible study, Youth Worship Service, Nuclear Disarmament Rally, reader, usher.
- Assigned leadership and clearly stated expectations, good preparation and organization, and open communication.
  —Poor organization and preparation for church barbeque, rap sessions without coordinator and set agenda, changing meeting plans at last minute, lack of communication about rally transportation.

It may be helpful to give each group a copy of the example or to post a copy where all can see it to use as a guide.

67

3. *10 Minutes*
   Gather back in the large group. Have the small groups share their value statements with the entire group.
4. *15 to 20 minutes*
   As you look at these sheets of values you have as a group, ask the group to compare this list with their statement of purpose. When the value statements and purpose statement are compatible, put your list in priority order. Select four goals which you feel will be manageable within your time frame.

   Some goals which might be suggested from the example are:
   —Develop and carry out service projects for people within our church and community.
   —Have monthly fellowship activities to get to know each other better and to meet more people from the church and community.
   —Plan and organize faith exploration events.
   —Have more youth serve on church budget and program committees, judicatory and national committees.
   Write the team's goals on newsprint.

Step 5: Stating Objectives

Objectives are direct, measurable actions which help toward accomplishing goals. They are the programs, projects, events and changes which bring the team closer to their goals.

Five characteristics should be used to test each objective to make sure that it is truly a workable objective. Using these five measurements helps to assure you that your objective has enough focus to be carried out well and easily. Is your objective:

> **S**pecific enough to be carried out? Does it have a **M**easurable outcome? Is it

Acceptable to the whole group? And
Realistic for your group to attempt? Is it
Timed for carrying out and completion?

Using the SMART system to test each objective keeps your
task manageable and possible.

Deciding on Objectives

1. *20 minutes*
   One way to go about determining the objectives is to divide
   the total group into small groups, one for each goal area.
   Ask the groups to look at and discuss their goal area. Then
   ask them to brainstorm as many objectives as possible that
   relate to their goal area. They should record on newsprint
   all of their suggestions.
2. *30 minutes*
   Have the group decide on the three ideas they all want the
   group to work on. Each of these should be a written objective statement. (Remember, be SMART.)
3. *30 minutes*
   Each group presents its ideas to the total group. Discuss
   each group of objectives and put in priority order those the
   team wants to work on.

As an example, in one youth empowerment project the
group decided to give priority to their first goal which was to
"have training events for youth leaders to help strengthen
youth ministry in the local church, the association and the
conference." Their objectives for this goal were:

1. Sponsor a series of three training events (fall, winter and
   spring) for a selected group of youth and adults for the
   purpose of experiencing personal Christian growth, learning specific skills to help lead local church youth groups,
   and gaining experiences in mission.

2. This group of trained youth and adults consequently will reach out and visit 3–5 churches in order to share its leadership skills with others.
3. This group will also lead programs for 3–5 local church cluster gatherings and weekend retreats.
4. These teams will be the core group to plan for and participate in both their church annual meetings and the judicatories annual meeting.
5. The team will gather and distribute information to all the churches in the judicatory on the denomination's position on peace and conscientious objection.

Step 6: Brainstorming Strategies

For each objective, a set of strategies needs to be listed. So many times a program or project gets bogged down because some detail in preparation has been overlooked. This may mean rushing around at the last minute to find refreshments for the meeting or calling around to find someone to lead devotions on the campout.

Strategies are the steps involved in reaching a specific objective, i.e., the jobs involved in planning and carrying out a program or project. Taking the time to outline these steps can mean the difference between a program that runs smoothly and one where details are thrown together at the last minute and the program looks it.

Deciding on these strategies involves some brainstorming by the total group or by the special committee in charge of each objective. Work on one objective at a time, or have small groups each work, on behalf of the team, on the development of strategies for one objective. The strategies should be listed in the sequence of steps needed to be taken to get from where you are to where you want to be.

Being thorough in these initial planning times and outlining all the strategies lead to a more smoothly run program and avoid last minute rushing to take care of forgotten details.

Step 7: The Timetable and Detail Chart

Setting up a timetable involves the placement of all of your objectives and strategies on a calendar which spans a particular phase. If you are planning for a three month period, you would take the objectives you have chosen and place them on the calendar on dates convenient to the group during that three-month time block. If you are planning for the entire year, your calendar would span a year and the objectives would be placed accordingly. You may want to make up a large calendar where your whole program year is visible at a glance. Post this in your meeting place.

The other variety of timetable which is beneficial to make is a What/How/By When/By Whom/Cost diagram. It is helpful in relieving some common concerns expressed by groups.

WHAT	HOW	BY WHEN	BY WHOM	COST

There are three common complaints of many youth ministry groups that can cause tension among the members and keep things from flowing merrily along. One such complaint is "A few people are doing all the work." This may not be the way the group intends to work; but without proper advance planning, it can happen. Another well known complaint is "We always end up doing everything at the last minute." This isn't necessarily bad, and some groups may enjoy working this way; but it can put a lot of pressure on those doing the work and create some tension as to whether everything really will get done in time. The third complaint usually goes something like, "If we'd known it was going to cost that much, we wouldn't have started it." Maybe this isn't one you hear quite so often; but many times when a project is finished, a group finds that the cost and effort they put into it wasn't really equal to the benefit that came from the end result, and that their time could have been better spent elsewhere.

The What/How/By When/By Whom/Cost Diagram is one way to minimize these problems.

The "Whats" are the working strategies that you outlined for each objective. Each of these is listed and a How, By When, By Whom, and Cost is decided on for each.

The "By When" is a time schedule. Assigning a time when certain strategies should be finished and following fairly close to this schedule help keep unfinished details from piling up at the last minute. Included in this should be a specified time for evaluation, reflection and celebration for each objective.

"How" is a short description of the steps needed to accomplish the strategies.

Choosing the people who will be responsible to work on each strategy is the "By Whom" section. This is very helpful in keeping the work evenly distributed.

"Cost" is self-explanatory. Estimating costs ahead of time helps give you a general idea of what percentage of your budget will be used on this objective and whether the particular strategy for that objective is worth the cost, and how much money you'll need to raise for it.

Following an outline such as this for major projects can be time and tension saving.

Working through the first seven steps of the planning process brings you to the point where you begin carrying out all of your objectives within your program year. The time you spend working through these first seven steps depends on the amount of time your group wants to spend. As was mentioned before, it is important to get a commitment from the group on the amount of time they are willing to spend in planning before you begin working on a schedule.

Below are two possible schedules for planning. Review these with your group and get a sense of the amount of time they want to work. Then use one of these as a guide to designing your own planning session.

If feasible, brainstorming strategies and work on timetables can be done at a regular meeting time following this planning session.

Weekend Retreat

Friday
7:30 p.m.	Orientation to the weekend
7:45	Group building (Getting acquainted and sharing yourself stages)
9:45	Theological reflection
10:00	Snacks

Saturday
9:30 a.m.	Group building (Revealing feelings stage)
10:15	Bible study
11:15	Break
11:30	Developing a statement of purpose
12:15	Break for lunch
1:30	Goal setting
3:00	Free time
5:30	Dinner
7:30	Outlining objectives
8:30	Setting up a timetable
9:00	Free time
11:30	Worship

Sunday
9:30 a.m.	Brainstorming strategies for each objective
10:00	What/How/By When/By Whom/Cost Diagram (Set time and place for evaluation, reflection, celebration.)
11:00	Worship
11:30	Pack to go home

73

Three Evenings of Planning

Evening One

7:00 p.m.	Theological reflection
7:15	Group building
9:15	Snack
9:30	Go home

Evening Two

7:00 p.m.	Developing a statement of purpose
7:45	Goal setting
9:15	Worship
9:30	Snacks
9:45	Go home

Evening Three

7:00 p.m.	Outlining objectives
7:45	Setting up a timetable
8:15	Brainstorming strategies for each objective
8:45	What/How/By When/By Whom/Cost Diagram (Set time for evaluation/reflection on each objective)
9:15	Worship
9:30	Snacks
9:45	Go home

Notes

1. Leslie Brandt, *Jesus/Now*. Concordia Publishing House, St. Louis, 1978. (p. 176–178.) Used by permission.
2. Brandt, ibid., p. 152–153. Used by permission.
3. Ginny Ward Holderness, *Youth Ministry: The New Team Approach* (John Knox Press: Atlanta, p. 107. Used by permission.
4. Ibid., p. 24.
5. Ibid., p. 22.
6. The idea for this exercise was developed in conversation with Lorin Cope.
7. *Youth Group Handbook,* Parish Life Press: Philadelphia, 1976. Used by permission.
8. Herman Ahrens, *Youth Magazine* (Philadelphia: United Church Press. Fall, 1977. Used by permission.

CHAPTER FIVE

On Our Way

Theoretically—if we practiced what we preached—this chapter would be a series of unmarked pages just standing by while you and the youth empowerment team implemented the plans you have devised so carefully. Now though, for better or for worse and despite theory, the overpowering value is ecology and thrift.

This chapter, therefore, describes some actions other youth teams have designed, to illustrate the kinds of results that can come from careful planning. Each action step was devised and implemented to meet a specific objective. Their inclusion here is as a potpourri of ideas meant to spark some of your own.

Communication

A Youth Empowerment Team in Ohio found that one major need area in their judicatory was for communication among youth in the churches. No method was available for local church youth groups to share ideas among themselves, or for them to easily find out what was happening on the regional level in youth ministry programming. The Team felt that improved communication of happenings plus the sharing of ideas and resources would be one way to enrich these churches' ministries.

Their answer to this concern was to begin the publication of a bimonthly newsletter for youth and youth leaders. Under the title of the "YET Gazette," the Team pulled together listings of those creative activities which were happenings in local churches in their conference. Varieties of program ideas were shared, as well as travelogs on work trips and study trips made by various groups from local churches. A resource listing which could be beneficial to programming appeared frequently. The newsletter often carried letters and articles written by young people outlining their concerns about some of the issues that their denomination was dealing with, both nationally and locally. Young people who attended the national denominational meeting wrote articles about their experiences.

When an interest was expressed for visiting other local churches within the judicatory, they introduced the "Swap It" column. A church youth group in Cleveland who was interested in visiting a rural area or in having a group visit them in Cleveland would share this information or invitation through the newsletter. They would then be contacted by interested readers. As a result, several successful "Swaps" were made as groups in different areas of Ohio met and got to know new people, new cities, and new lifestyles during a weekend exchange.

A checklist of upcoming dates for youth rallies, training events and committee meetings was also included. Reminders of upcoming happenings within the larger church, such as annual meetings, increased youth participation in these events. And by highlighting the need for young people on judicatory committees and commissions and by outlining the work of these groups, many youth were made aware of their existence and placed their names into nomination for these working groups. Several were subsequently elected.

This team found that a newsletter could open up many new avenues for enriching the ministry of their constituency. People were anxious to share ideas and even more anxious to read them. As this paper reached out to more people, they felt more a part of the larger ministry of the denomination.

Community

The churches in the Southeast Conference of one denomination are few and far between. Less than one hundred churches are spread across Alabama, Tennessee, Georgia and part of South Carolina. So when the Youth Core looked at options for building a feeling of community among the young people in their churches, they were faced with a distance problem which was unique. One answer was to hold "Pop-Ins" in local churches in different parts of their Conference.

At a "Pop-In", carloads of young people and adult advisors from churches within a hundred mile radius brought their sleeping bags and converged on one local church for the weekend. They slept on the church floor Friday and Saturday nights and usually had their meals in the church too. The purpose was just to get together, meet new people, see old friends, share faith journeys, and have fun. Youth from that local church or members of the Youth Core coordinated the program.

The program could range anywhere from discussions about faith, lifestyles and sexuality to New Games tournaments and tours of the local area. Sometimes getting acquainted, group building and human relations activities were planned. Music and songfests were usually integral parts. Worship was led by members of the local group, and they often worshiped with the congregation on Sunday morning. At the end of one event, one participating church volunteered to host the next one.

In the Southeast Conference they saw a need to develop an identity and community among young people in their far-reaching churches. One of their solutions was to develop an event with a consistency of style, values, and interest, in an accessible location within a wide geographic radius. It worked wonders.

Service

As the Ohio Youth Empowerment Team traveled around the state working with local churches, they were known to be great supporters of service projects and social concern. Groups were often challenged to reach out into their community and beyond to become aware of the needs of others. Suggestions for various service projects and worktrips were readily forthcoming.

Their sincere concern was questioned, however, at one point by a group who asked what service project the Team themselves were involved in. Not only, it was said, would a YET service project truly demonstrate their concern for service, but this particular youth group, and they suggested others too, would be interested in helping with such a project.

It was from this challenge and the commitment to living out their philosophy for service that "Operation: CHORKLE" was born.

It was known that for some communities in Appalachia, the nearest library was fifty miles away. This was practically inaccessible for most of the people. The need for a library which was more readily available for local residents was one concern of the staff of an interdenominational mission project working to improve conditions in one area of Tennessee.

The Youth Empowerment Team undertook a project to collect five thousand books to start a local library in this area. The project title, CHORKLE, stood for Collecting Helps Others Receive a Knowledgeable Lifelong Education.

A challenge went out to the young people of churches within their regional area to participate in this service project with them. Youth groups were asked to collect new and used books from people in their churches, and from their local libraries, schools and communities. Drop centers were located at eight places across the state where groups could bring the books they had collected.

The response was amazing. Youth groups rallied around the state. They collected used books and raised money to buy new ones. In addition, several senior citizen centers who had heard about the project also responded, as did some schools who were willing to donate overflow textbooks and library duplicates. When a major newspaper decided to publicize the project, people joined in from several other areas.

The drop centers overflowed. Young people loaded boxes of books into cars and hauled them to Columbus, where they loaded them onto large trucks. The Youth Empowerment Team with the dedicated help of several young people and adults transported them to Deer Lodge, Tennessee, where they were unloaded by local young people into the community center. There they were inspected, sorted, and the process of cataloguing was begun by a volunteer librarian. They were eventually placed in three centers in two counties.

Over ten thousand books were transported to Deer Lodge—twice the amount hoped for—a literal snowball of youth enthusiasm.

Events

To have a youth ministry gathering to which all the young people and adult leaders in all the churches in their area would be invited was the goal of several youth empowerment models. To present and promote an event which would build community among youth and adults of a particular region, which would highlight and share ideas of youth ministry happenings, and which would help increase the involvement of young people in the churches was a major challenge undertaken by many teams. Several of these events which happened were ecumenical; some were denominational. Many were regional; some were cluster gatherings. They were different in format, topic, style and size. But they were alike in enthusiasm, excitement, enjoyment and eagerness for repetition.

For some young people, attending these events was the first time that they had experienced an activity beyond their local church. For those young people who had been the dreamers, the planners and the taskmakers, it was a chance to celebrate with other people in their area and to share with those others some dreams of what the church is and can be.

Focus of events ranged from workshops on leadership skills to sessions on communication, to discussing faith and lifestyles. Size was anywhere from fifty to three hundred. Places were churches, camps, state fair grounds, and college campuses. The similarity among all of them was that they were planned and carried out by youth with the help of a core group of adults.

One such event was planned by a group of young people who wanted to explore the effect that mass media has on our lifestyle, on our self-image and on our faith. They chose a weekend in November and decided to hold their event at their denominational conference center. They titled it "Media Mania". An associate professor from the nearby state university was asked to come in as their major speaker and program leader.

As part of the planning, the committee outlined and discussed the major tasks that would be involved. The following leadership positions were decided upon and responsibilities assigned for each.

WHO	RESPONSIBLE FOR
Overall coordinators	Chairing planning committee, contacting resource people, making all announcements at event itself and being the contact persons for questions and concerns during the event

Worship leader	Planning all worship sessions
Music coordinator	Leading all singing and helping plan music for worship
On-site maintenance person	Organizing all room arrangements and handling any problems related to the site
Recreation/free time overseer	Coordinating optional activities and games during free time
Program leader	Planning and leading major program times
Group building leader	Leading get acquainted and group building activities
Workshop leaders	Leading special interest workshops as assigned
Dance coordinators	Coordinating dance/entertainment times and arranging for necessary equipment
Film coordinator	Securing films, projector, and screens. Setting up and showing films
Meal coordinator	Arranging for hoppers for each meal and for table grace for each meal
Registrar/room assignments	Handling pre-event registration process, coordinating on site registration and assigning rooms to participants
Publicity person	Preparing and sending out publicity pieces and registration forms. Sending out followup letter to registrants on what to bring, etc.

Nature/hiking enthusiast	Providing opportunities for participants to explore the outdoor setting of the conference center
Resource/display arranger	Recruiting display of youth ministry resources and for displays from local colleges
Night patrol	Walking around the site after lights out and making sure all is secure.

In making up the schedule, the planning committee tried to provide several options for activities for people as well as plenty of free time. They recognized the motivation of people to stay up late at events like this so they set a late curfew and started later in the morning with an optional breakfast. They realized that many problems occur at events like this because expectations of the leadership and the participants are not clarified. So they programmed this into the schedule at the beginning, and they made sure that each person had a copy of the schedule.

When it happened, the event looked like this.

Media Mania

When	*What*	*Where*
Friday evening 8:00–9:00 p.m.	Registration/Nametags	Lodge— fireplace area
	Other options:	Lodge—
	Listen to music	Dining area
	Watch funny films	Meeting House
	Move into cabins	
	Hiking	Meet outside Lodge at 8:15
	Visit display area	Fellowship room #1

82

When	What	Where
9:00–10:00	Group Building	Lodge
10:00–10:15	Introduction, Welcome, Outline of schedule, Expectations and Questions	Lodge
10:15–10:45	Snack	Lodge—dining area
10:45–11:30	Film Introduction to Media Theme	Lodge
11:30–12:00	Worship	Lodge
12:00–3:00	Free Time	Lodge and Meeting House only
3:00 a.m.	Lights out! All in cabins!	

Saturday

When	What	Where
9:00–9:45 a.m.	Continental Breakfast	Lodge—dining area
9:45–10:00	Group Singing	Lodge
10:00–10:30	Worship	Lodge
10:30–12:30	Program: How media affects our lives	Lodge
12:45	Hoppers report for lunch set up	Lodge—dining area
1:00	Lunch	Lodge—dining area
1:45–2:00	Group Singing	Lodge
2:00–4:00	Program: How can we respond to media?	Lodge
4:00–6:00	Free Time options: Hiking	Meet outside Lodge at 4:30
	New Games Tournament	Meadow
5:45	Hoppers report for dinner set up	Lodge—dining area
6:00	Dinner	Lodge
7:00–7:30	Worship	Lodge

When	What	Where
7:30–8:00	Announcements and Information Summer camp information Youth Task Force information Larger church opportunities Outline of evening's activities	Lodge
8:15–9:15	Options I Bible Study	Fellowship Room #2
	"Godspell"—Community Church Youth Players	Meeting House
	Idea Fair: sharing time to get ideas for your youth group	Fellowship Room #1
	Square Dancing	Lodge
	Discussion and Presentation by those who attended the denominational convention	Staff House Lounge
9:30–10:30	Options II Bible Study (repeat)	Fellowship Room #2
	Godspell (repeat)	Meeting House
	Jam Session: Singing with guitars	Staff House Lounge
	Square Dancing	Lodge
10:30	Snack	Lodge
11:00	Options Disco Dancing	Lodge
	Hiking	Meet outside lodge at 11:00
	Funny Films	Meeting House

When	What	Where
	Free time	Lodge, Fellowship House and Cabins only
3:00 a.m.	Lights out! All in cabins!	
Sunday Morning		
9:00–9:45 a.m.	Continental Breakfast Clean up cabins	Lodge
9:45–10:15	Meet in regional groups to find out what is happening in youth ministry in your regions	
10:15–10:30	Group Singing	Lodge
10:30–12:30	Program: How does media affect our faith?	Lodge
12:45	Hoppers report to set up lunch	Lodge— dining area
1:00	Lunch Clean up cabins!	Lodge
1:45	Closing Worship	Lodge
2:30	Head for home	

Three hundred youth and adults attended "Media Mania". Evaluations were positive in favor of the schedule and activities. But most comments reflected a joy at getting together with young people and adults from other churches, meeting new people, seeing old friends, sharing ideas, celebrating their faith together and finding new ways of being the church.

Themes

The above programs and projects were used by various youth empowerment teams. Many other ideas exist for you to try based on the concerns and interests of your own group. Look again at the list of issues your group feels that the church should respond to in the world today. What thoughts come to your mind for action? An extended list has been put together of issues that have been discussed by other groups of concerned youth. Maybe these will stimulate more ideas for your team.

Some Issues of Concern to Young People

Faith healing	Overpopulation	Political spying
Islam	Hinduism	Beliefs of Quakers
Housing	Juvenile delinquency	Birth defects
Prison reform	Ecology	Use and abuse of power
Affluence	Science and faith	Capital punishment
Hunger	Conflicts between parents and teens	War and peace
Conscientious objection		Leadership development
Human sexuality	Poverty	Racism
Making ethical decisions	Drug abuse	Alcoholism
	Disarmament	
Mental illness	Death	Divorce
Marriage	Death with dignity	Child abuse
Suicide	Native Americans	Medical ethics
Extra-sensory perception	Role of women	Role of men
Exorcism	Handicaps	Aging
Charismatic Christianity	Anger and violence	Consumerism

		Nuclear power/ weapons
Genetic engineering	Meditation	Interfaith marriage
Evangelism	Money management	Career exploration
Youth unemployment	Youth crime	Reincarnation
Welfare systems	Emotionally disturbed children	Minorities
Civil rights	The family	Celebrative worship
Militarism	Communication	Communal living
Competition	Anxiety	Adoption

Activities beyond the local church are often sponsored through the national denominational offices for youth. Several denominations sponsor national opportunities for young people as well as international travel programs. Many have activities for youth as part of their denominational conferences.

For information about activities sponsored through your denomination, see your pastor or regional minister.

CHAPTER SIX

Evaluation and Celebration

By now, if your group has gone through the planning process and engaged in action, you may recognize yourself in the following description:

You've gotten to know one another. You feel a great sense of group unity and purpose. You've worked hard for several months, first discussing who you were, what you needed, and what you wanted to be about, then carrying out programs and activities: worship services and evening vespers, congregational activities and judicatory events, weekend retreats and evening meetings, social times and work projects, Bible studies and spaghetti dinners. Some times were rough. Other times were fun. One day you wondered if anyone else besides you was doing any of the work. But then you were amazed that the backpacking retreat ran smoothly without you.

Now it's over and it is worth all those extra hours everyone put in. You've grown as a person and as a Christian. You feel enriched by some of the experiences and a little wiser from others. Now it is time to evaluate and celebrate all those actions, learnings, and experiences.

Evaluation

Evaluation is one of the most often forgotten and neglected elements of the planning process. Whether in the glow of success, the agony of defeat, or somewhere in between, the thought of evaluation gets lost. Yet it is one of the most important steps. The learnings gleaned from these intentional evaluations of your team life and work are the insights and sparks for future planning. We grow by learning from our experiences, and by using those learnings creatively and practically. Evaluation involves looking at what has happened, highlighting the accomplishments, discovering the learnings from the experience and outlining ways to put these to use in the future life of the organization.

Three areas need to be looked at when you are doing evaluation. The first area involves organization. How well were you organized and prepared to get the job done? The second area is method. How did things go? What were the strategies involved in doing the program or activity? Did the people involved understand what was supposed to be done? And did they do it? The third area is results. How well did the project turn out? Was it what you planned? Did it contribute toward accomplishing your goal?

As you evaluate keep these three elements in mind. Through looking at these areas, you can get a clearer picture of how and why things worked or didn't work, where your strong points were, and what areas needed more work. You can also determine whether your achievements were what you expected and in what ways they met the needs stated in the goal.

Evaluation should take place at the conclusion of each event (this also includes evaluating group meetings at some point) and at the conclusion of your program season. The consistency and thoroughness of these evaluations are important if you are to get a complete understanding of all three areas. Means, methods, and persons to do these evaluations can vary.

Single Event Evaluation

The chairperson and/or the task group assigned for a single event may be the one/s asked to do the evaluation on that specific activity. Or it may be more beneficial that the total group involved in the event participate in the process. Sometimes both are relevant. For example, after a group retreat looking at faith exploration, it would be valuable to get feedback from all who were there about how they felt about the content and the location and if their expectations were met; at the conclusion of a fund-raising airplane wash at your local airport (much like a car wash at the local service station), it is usually enough for the organizer/coordinator and any other planners to reflect on its success. For a regional youth event, the evaluative comments from the participants as well as those of the planning committee and the leadership are all necessary information for a thorough evaluation and helpful background for future planning.

Several types of simple evaluations can be used for single events. Below are three examples.

- At the conclusion of the activity, ask everyone to shout out adjectives which describe their feelings about the experience. These should be encouraged to cover the spectrum of feelings, both positive and negative. All these adjectives are written on newsprint for everyone to see. Just a series of descriptive words can give a wide range of reactions to an event which can provide some indication of the affective response.
- One commonly used and very helpful evaluation involves each person responding on a sheet of paper to three major questions:

—What three things did you like best about this event and why?

—What three things did you enjoy the least and why?

—What should be done differently when planning this type of event again?

The answers are compiled by the planning committee into an overall evaluative statement.

• A more detailed evaluation would ask about specific elements of the experience. It could include open ended, multiple choice questions, or statements to be rated by number. This evaluation would have to be tailored for the situation. Questions would focus around the three areas of evaluation: organization, method and results. A sample evaluation follows:

1. The faith exploration sessions were: (circle one)

boring okay interesting above my helped me learn
head more about my faith

2. The worship sessions were _____ because _____.

3. The role play exercise gave me an understanding of the meaning of the parable: (circle one number)

1   2   3   4   5   6   7
a little   a lot

4. One addition I would have made to the weekend: (circle one)

more free more planned longer content better (other)
time recreation sessions meals _____

Each participant fills out the evaluation form. All the answers are compiled by the planning committee into one evaluative report.

Periodic Evaluations

As each evaluation gives you the learnings and insights for the next activity, so the evaluation of your total program season gives you some direction and concerns for planning for the next season. Looking back over the total calendar of activities and events, programs and projects, you gain an overview on how well you met your goals, how realistic those goals were, and the learnings which will enrich your program in the future. Only by doing this will you intentionally facilitate the growth of the group that you desire.

Participants in these evaluation sessions should include, at least, representatives, participants, and planners from each of the single events. Most likely this session will be separate from any other activity. A whole afternoon or evening devoted to evaluation is not too much. Begin with some type of getting in touch activity. This is especially important if some in attendance are not constant attenders. Some simple activities which could begin people thinking about evaluation are:

1. In small groups of six or eight, have each person share the most meaningful experience that has happened to him or her while engaged in some activity or program of the group this season.
2. In small groups, ask each person to share a brief story about a time when she or he felt ministered to during this program season. Include feelings about this ministry.
3. In small groups, ask each person to share a brief story about a time when he or she ministered to someone else during their times together.
4. During a ten- to fifteen-minute period of *total silence,* provide participants with a sheet of paper and crayons and ask them to illustrate in words or pictures their learnings and experiences from the past program season. A variation of this would be to make a collage in words and pictures taken

from magazines and newspapers. At the end of the time period, participants share and interpret their creation for the rest of the group.

This review and sharing should be followed by an explanation of the purpose of evaluation, describing how the information gathered at this meeting will influence future plans.

Evaluating the Planning and Implementation

List all the activities that have happened during your program season. Be sure to include one labeled "Group Meetings" to designate the business meetings of your group. These need evaluation too. Note by each activity the goal to which it relates. Post this list of activities and a list of goal statements where they are visible to all.

Divide into groups of four and assign each group three or four activities to evaluate. Each group should appoint a recorder. Any available evaluation reports on specific activities should be given to the small group assigned to those activities. It is helpful if members of the small groups have participated in the activities assigned to them.

Each small group should focus on one activity at a time. For this activity the groups should discuss the following questions. The recorder should note down the group's answers.

- Did the activity meet the stated goal? How? or Why not?
- What were the learnings from the activity? Emphasize both positive and negative learnings.
- How can we incorporate these learnings into our future planning in a positive way?

Give the groups adequate time to discuss each activity in depth.

When you reconvene in the total group, each small group should report its responses to the questions. Give time after each report for further contributions or clarifications by the total group. One person should be recording the responses to question three on newsprint for the entire group to see.

After each group has reported, open the floor for other positive learnings the group feels are important to future planning and growth of the group. It is these learnings that will benefit the future planning of your group and which are the valuable outcome of an evaluation process.

It may be helpful to give this long list of learnings to a small group to be combined, clarified and focused. Or you may feel that their present form is concise enough. This final list should then be typed up and distributed to each member for use at the future planning session for your next program season.

Celebration

Celebration is like the applause after the final curtain of a good play. This applause has a two-fold purpose: to express the joy and appreciation for the experience, and to show thanks and gratitude to all those who were a part of creating and sustaining that experience. Without the final applause, the play would not seem complete. Without the worship celebration, the planning and implementation are not complete. The applause/celebration is directed to each other and to the power source of the community—God.

Any type of worship celebration that you do should include both of these elements: the expression of joy and support for one another, and the expression of gratitude and commitment to God.

The Youth Ministry Resources listed in Chapter Nine (page 00) include several books on worship. Some give the outline of a service and suggest content. Several include prayer and meditation as parts of worship; others involve interpreting and celebrating our faith through creative storytelling. Your local pastor, worship committees, and musicians will be able to suggest other resources.

As you plan your celebration, some of the examples below may be helpful.

Youth Life in Technicolor

Prepare a slide show with pictures of as many of your activities as possible. An official team photographer should be designated to record planning meetings, the team en route and at each event. A variety of pictures including the faces of as many members and variety of events as possible is best.

Set up these slides in a chronological sequence preparing a script to accompany them which highlights happenings, learnings, growth change, and awakenings which were a part of your ministry. It might be similar to a "This is Youth Life at First Community Church."

The slides could also be arranged to focus on each individual member with the script highlighting his or her contributions to the life and ministry of the group.

The addition of some music would be the final touch.

Circle of Gifts

Too often the positive reinforcement which we give to those around us is little and rare. As we get caught up in the hustle and bustle of activity, we forget to recognize and celebrate the talents, large and small, which people contribute to our ongoing ministry. A deliberate moment for affirming each participant with the quality of their merits is never wasted.

Have everyone sit in a large circle. Each person is asked to spend a few minutes concentrating on each of the other members of the group and the talents, skills, and joys which that person has brought to the group through his/her participation in it. As part of their reflecting, each person must come up with a gift (either real or imaginary) for each other person in the group which is somehow related to the talents, skills, and joys that that other person brought to the group. This reflec-

95

tion should be done in silence so that all ideas are kept original. All gifts are asked to be serious and sincere.

When everyone has decided on the gifts they want to give, begin by concentrating on one person. All others in the group should present their gifts one at a time to that person, explaining the reason behind the gift to the entire group. The person receiving the gifts should receive them in silence responding only with a Thank You to the group at the end.

Yes, Amen

Each person who has been involved in the ministry of your youth empowerment model most likely has one or two experiences which are particularly valuable to her/him as growing or sharing experiences. These are part of what made the entire ministry meaningful. Sharing these with the entire group can be a valuable means of celebrating their ministry and focusing on the personal experiences which made it worthwhile.

As part of your worship celebration, ask anyone who wishes to share a special time when they felt ministered to or to share something they are thankful for within the group. After each person shares his or her experience, the total group responds with a positive thank you for this sharing by singing:

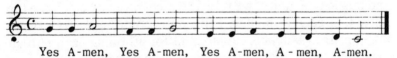

Yes A-men, Yes A-men, Yes A-men, A-men, A-men.

The most meaningful and creative worship celebration is built around issues and concerns which are a part of your group's experience together. As you plan your worship celebration, look at moments that stand out in your memory about your times together. What are special contributions made by different people? What are those things for which you are most thankful?

Compose a song. Write a prayer. Tell a story. Make your celebration a part of you and make it a tribute to God.

CHAPTER SEVEN

Leadership—
A Divided House

Imagine, if you will, a retreat for adults and youth involved in youth ministry. During the opening, getting-acquainted period, a series of statements are made to start the group reflecting on how they feel about ministry with youth. Each person is asked to move to the right side of the room if they agree with the statement and to the left side if they disagree. The barrage of statements causes stirs of movement back and forth: "I feel younger adults work better with youth than older adults." "You should let an event fail if the people planning it have neglected to do the work needed." "I feel human sexuality is an important issue for the church to help its youth understand." Some statements cause a majority of people to move to the left; others cause them to move to the right. All get spirited comments. The last statement causes some lively discussion, "I believe that the ability to be a good leader and to work well with people is an inborn quality, not a learned one."

How do you feel about this last one? Would you move to

the right or to the left? A group in Portland, Maine was split almost evenly. When everyone had committed themselves to one side or the other, people from both sides mixed together into small groups to talk about their responses in more depth. Do leadership skills and the ability to work well with people come naturally, or are they learned? You might try discussing this in your group.

Journal Jottings VII

Think about the following questions. What makes people good leaders? What are those traits that they have which make them stand out? What are your own attitudes and ideas of a valuable leader?

On a sheet of paper, write this phrase at the top: "To me a good leader is. . . ." Now complete this sentence with as many adjectives and descriptive phrases as you can think of. When you fill up that sheet, start on another.

When finished, your list may look something like this.

tactful
friendly
concerned about the welfare of the group above personal welfare
capable of keeping a group on target in discussions
able to interpret and interrupt the group when necessary
knows how to enable the group to express their ideas
never forces his/her ideas on the group
tries to involve as many people as possible in the planning and working of the group
responsible to get things done
sensitive to the dynamics of the group
fun to be with
shares leadership responsibility with others rather than trying to do everything alone

has Christian beliefs
is supportive of other members of the group
tries to keep aware of what is happening in all areas of the
    group's work
assertive
understanding
open to new ideas
has commitment to the work of the group

Maybe then the answer to the question about natural or learned leadership skills is two-fold. We all have skills and talents to bring to any job when we begin it. These skills and talents bring with them the potential for developing broader skills. Thus, you work with those talents which are natural and use these natural traits to expand your learned skills. The most rewarding part about working with a group of people is the variety of talents and skills which that group presents.

Each person is unique and has special talents in which he or she excels and other areas in which her or his skills are not as strong. In analyzing the working of people with a group, these special talents can be divided into four categories: Thinker, Doer, Organizer, Feeler. A word about each category.

The *Thinker* is one who is always bubbling over with ideas. This person often has an idea for a program or a place to go or a speaker to engage. Seldom at a loss for possibilities, the thinker is a dreamer.

The *Feeler* is the interpreter of the group. Often he or she helps to bring into a more realistic context the dreams of the Thinker. The Feeler has a good grasp of the dynamics and workings of the group. She or he can suggest how the variety of gifts and skills of the different members can be used in planning and implementation.

The *Organizer* tells you how to go about getting things done. When putting together the steps in planning, the Organizer is at his or her best. She or he can outline the best process for working out the ideas of the Feeler. Pulling together the strategies for action and setting them into a timetable is often done by the Organizer.

The *Doer* gets the job done. When all is said and done, the Doer is the one seen putting the chairs away, paying the bills, or cooking the spaghetti. You can count on the Doer to follow through with the leg work and the details.

As we examine the leadership styles of our team members—including ourselves—we often can identify those who excel or have strength in a particular area. Note, however, that no one is exclusively a Doer, or a Thinker, or a Feeler, or an Organizer. Each of us has some capability in each of these categories, though we may be stronger or more dominant in one area than another.

Journal Jottings VIII

Using the four categorizes presented above, how would you describe your leadership style?

Think about yourself for a moment. Are you more of a Doer or a Feeler? Do you do better as an Organizer or as a Thinker? Possibly assigning percentages to yourself can give you a better perspective.

ME		YOU	
Thinker	25%	Thinker	——— %
Feeler	45%	Feeler	——— %
Organizer	10%	Organizer	——— %
Doer	20%	Doer	——— %
	———		———
	100%		100%

Asking a friend to describe you in this way can be a very awakening experience. Occasionally their perceptions of you vary considerably from the way you see yourself.

Realizing the existence of these areas and recognizing where they are strongest in you and in your group can help as you plan activities or assign committees.

Imagine yourself in a typical committee meeting. The group is trying to decide on a method for raising money for a charity. They want an activity that will bring in money and that will also draw attention to their particular cause. Terry Thinker suggests having a Teeter-Totter Marathon where the teeter-totter is placed on a flatbed wagon and hauled to various public places during the marathon to increase visibility. Everyone responds enthusiastically to her idea; but when it comes to action, no one wants to be in charge. So Carl Chairman puts Terry Thinker in charge of the Teeter-Totter Marathon because she came up with the idea. Terry reluctantly agrees. (Ring any bells?)

Terry Thinker has a chart that looks like this:

Thinker	45%
Feeler	35%
Organizer	10%
Doer	10%

She has a lot of ideas to share and has a good grasp on the dynamics of the group, but she is less skilled at organizing and doing. Any guesses on the outcome of the Marathon?

This example is not to say that your group should make a chart on each member and gauge responsibilities according to areas of strength. The point here is that we need to assess our skills and work to highlight our strengths and to build up the areas where we are weaker. A more workable method to use in our example would have been for the chairman to put Olga Organizer in charge of the Marathon and to ask Terry Thinker to be her assistant. Thus, Terry would be able to improve her organizing skills by working with someone strong in organizing and by beginning with minimal responsibilities and working toward more.

A group who often has the same people in leadership positions may not have recognized the potential that exists for enabling leadership in other members through building up their skills gradually.

Putting to use your greatest potential in an empowerment model requires you to recognize the skills and talents of each member, highlight these strengths and work to expand new areas. In this way you maximize individual talents and affirm the worth of each member while helping them grow.

CHAPTER EIGHT

Training Models for Youth Empowerment Leadership

Many Youth Empowerment Teams have as a goal the organizing of training events. These events emphasize youth ministry leadership skills. The following ideas for organizing a training event and the outlines of events that other groups have sponsored may be helpful to you as you plan for your own.

Training events in programming and leadership skills provide people with opportunities and experiences for affirming and expanding their talents in the company of others who are concerned about youth ministry. A supportive community is an essential element of youth ministry training. Training in youth ministry involves the learning of new skills, improvement of existing skills, opportunities to test and practice these skills, and to reflectively evaluate our experiences within a community of love and support and to celebrate the presence of the Holy Spirit in our work.

The Six Basics

Training events for youth ministry skills come in all shapes, sizes, and styles. You may never find two where the format is exactly alike. However, on closer examination you might see that in some form or another they all include six basic elements.

- Introduction/Orientation
- Group Building
- Content
- Informal Time
- Feedback/Evaluation
- Worship/Celebration

All six elements should be included in a well planned event.

Introduction and Orientation

This section gives the overview or the reasons for the event. It should answer the question, Why are we here? During this time the purpose and goals of the event are described; an outline of the schedule is presented and questions related to it are answered; expectations of participants are clarified; and the leaders and members of the Planning Committee are introduced. A brief time can also be spent looking ahead at what some hopes and dreams are as follow-up for this event.

Group Building.

This is the time spent meeting new people and getting to know old friends better. During this time participants goe from feeling like one among a room full of strange faces to one among a community of friends. This element is very important—an atmosphere of openness, acceptance and Christian love promotes sharing and learning.

Content

This is where the direct learning and sharing of skills occur. It can take the form of workshops, keynote addresses, open discussion sessions, practical experiences, learning center experiences, and many others. The specific topics are dependent on the needs and interests of those people who will be involved in the event. A list of possible topics to be covered might include the following:

- Music
- Communication Skills
- Worship Skills
- Cults
- Careers/Vocational Planning
- Planning
- Evangelism
- Values Clarification
- Teens and Parents

- Bible Study
- Group Building
- Faith Exploration
- Drama and Dance
- Clowning
- Human Sexuality
- Workcamping
- Creative Programming

- Creativity
- Denominational Identity
- Outdoor Ministry
- Resources
- Media in Ministry
- Service Projects
- Adults Working with Youth
- Peer Relationships

Informal Time

This is the break time, recreation time or just time to catch your breath, relax and digest all the information that you have been taking in.

Feedback and Evaluation

The value of training events is minimal if they do not meet the needs of those who are attending. Evaluation and feedback provide information from participants about how well ideas were presented, whether what is learned is useful to one's ministry and what could have been done better. Evaluations, when constructed thoughtfully and received openly, can provide good ideas and directions for future events.

Worship/Celebration

This is the period of time for reflecting on the Christian bond which brings the group together. Thanks is offered to the God who makes all things possible and to each other for sharing gifts with the group and contributing to this ministry.

The Planning Key

Planning your own training event is a long process. But it is more manageable if you break it down into a series of steps and tasks. Whether you are planning a training event to be held for youth leaders and adult leaders from local churches in your region or for an intense training for a youth empowerment team, the general series of steps and tasks are much the same.

1. Determine the needs and interests of your constituency.
2. Determine a time frame for your event.
3. Outline the elements of the event and where they fit into your time frame.
4. Select content areas which relate to the needs and interests of participants.
5. Explore possible resources and leadership.
6. Assign tasks and responsibilities.
7. Look at evaluation and future follow-up.

The following instrument was designed as a worksheet for groups who are planning for a youth ministry training event. It gives more detailed ways for working through these seven steps.[1] Use it as a tool for planning your training event.

PLanning Key Worksheet[1]

Constituency: Needs and Interests

Who are we planning for? (youth, adults, pastors, others)

What are the needs of youth in your area: family needs, school and career needs, faith needs, etc.?

What are the questions that adult leaders of youth in your local churches are asking?

The thing that would be most helpful to the youth ministry program in my congregation right now is. . . .

Time Frame of the Event

What days of the week would be the best time frame for your constituency to attend an event?

How much time will you need to meet the needs and interests of your participants?

Examples of possible time frames:
   One-day workshop
   Three week nights
   Overnight event
   Two or three multiple weekends
   Other?

Elements of the Event

What are the elements that are important components of any event?

Following are some important elements and some examples of how they might fit into time frame models:

Elements to be included in all models:
1. Introduction/
   Orientation
2. Group Building
3. Content
4. Break
   (Informal Time)
5. Feedback/Evaluation
6. Worship Celebration

One Day Workshop
   9:00–9:30 a.m. Registration
   9:30–10:15 Introduction & Group Building
   10:15–10:30 Break
   10:30–12:30 Workshops/Learning Center Time
   12:30–1:45 Lunch
   1:45–3:45 Workshops
   3:45–4:00 Break
   4:00–4:15 Evaluation/Feedback
   4:15–4:30 Worship
   4:30 Go Home

3 Weeknights
    7:00–7:30 p.m. Gather, Get Acquainted
    7:30–9:30 Content
                Keynote
                Workshops
                Learning Centers
                Experiencing
    9:30–9:45 Worship
    9:45–10:00 Snacks (Optional)
    [9:45—evaluation (last night)]

Overnight Retreat
First Evening:
        7:30 p.m.–8:30 p.m. Registration
        8:30–9:30 Introduction and Group Building
        9:30–10:15 Keynote
        10:15–11:00 Refreshments
        11:00 Worship
Second Day:
        8:30 a.m. Breakfast
        9:30–12:00 Workshops/Learning Center time
        12:30 Lunch
        1:30–4:00 Workshops
        4:00–4:15 Break
        4:15–4:30 Feedback/Evaluation
        4:30–5:00 Worship

Decisions

A Checklist
What else needs doing?

What	How	By When	By Whom	Cost
Publicity				
Travel Pool				
Registration Process				
Room & Board/ Refreshments				
Reserve Youth Ministry Mobile Resource Library				
Coordinate Learning Centers				
Coordinate on-site needs and arrangements				

Content of the Event

What content *areas* do we need to include that will meet the needs and interests of our constituency?

What are the goals and the objectives of our event? (At the end of this event people will be able to. . . .

How do these content areas fit into our chosen time frame?

Resources and Leadership

Who are the people? Where is the place? What are the books, movies, magazines? Which learning centers do we use?

Who could be our workshop leaders?

Workshop	Possible Leaders

Leader Group Building: _____

Music Leader: _____

Worship Leader: _____

Keynoter: _____

What books, films, magazines, music, audio visuals do we want to make available? (Check the Youth Ministry Resource list in Chapter 9).

Who will enlist the resource people?

Who will secure the other resources needed?

Where are possible sites for our event?

   Needs we have:
      Small group rooms
      Large meeting room
      Geographically central
      Others?

   Options for sites:

Who will arrange for the site?

Evaluation, Re-entry, Future

What are important things we will want to know in evaluation of this event?

Who will handle the evaluation process?

How can you help participants to take all the learnings back home most effectively?

(For example, participants reflect on and discuss:

1. Who else can use these information/skills in your local church?

2. Where and how can you best share the things you learned at this event?)

What future plans does this group need to think about after the event?

Sample Training Designs

The variables that rise to shape a training event are numerous: place, time, location, focus, people, intent, needs, and so on. All of these combine to make each event unique. Following are two samples for training events which were designed for denominational youth empowerment projects. Each is different because the variables were different. Each was effective for the purpose intended. Following the previous planning outline for developing your own training event can lead you to one that is unique to your own model. Looking through these may give you some additional ideas.

Moravian Youth Empowerment Team's Training Design

The Moravian Youth Empowerment Team Project involved the training of five regional teams, each consisting of five youth and an adult advisor. The purpose of the YET's was to enhance youth ministry in the local congregations and to focus the attention of the church on the need for greater youth involvement in the total life of the church. The objectives of the YET were:

• To communicate with youth.

- To encourage effective youth participation in the local congregation.
- To share models/alternatives for local ministry.
- To aid in the evaluation of a local congregation's youth ministry.
- To facilitate youth/adult dialogues on youth needs, youth involvement in the church and on the role of adults working with youth.
- To educate youth concerning the structure and the functioning of the church as an institution.

As a means of carrying out these objectives, the teams participated in regional youth events, participated in the planning process of the regional youth councils, and worked directly with several local congregations. The format and content of the week-long training event for the Moravian Youth Empowerment Teams focused on developing of strengthening the skills needed to accomplish the objectives. The training was to include goal setting; group process; group building; worship and study times; plus a look at the Moravian Church, its history, structure and traditions, and how the YET could tie into the structures. In addition to the teams, various denominational and regional staff people participated in the training, as well as other youth delegates. Their week together looked like this.

First Day
   Dinner: Opening of training
   7:00: Total Group Building
   9:30: Worship
Second Day
   Breakfast
   9:00: Youth Ministry Concept and Philosophy
   Lunch
   1:30: Cross Section Group Building
   Free Time

Dinner

7:00: Regional Groups meet for reflection and starting on building the purpose and goal setting

9:30: Worship

Third Day

Breakfast

9:00: What are Group Leadership Techniques?

Lunch

Free Time

3:00: What is that which is Moravian?
    Liturgy, worship, customs, and practices

Dinner

7:00: Regional groups continue goal setting

9:30: Worship

Fourth Day

Breakfast

9:00: Communication Skills
    More time for regional groups

Lunch

2:00: Resources. Look at Youth Ministry Resources gathered, other bibliographies and exchange ideas on how to find resources

Dinner

7:00: Sharing of regional goals and models

9:30: Worship

Fifth Day

Breakfast

9:00: Commissioning of team members
    Closing celebration

United Church of Christ: Southeast Conference Youth Core Training Design

The Youth Core is a group of youth and adults concerned about empowering youth ministry in the local church. The purpose of the Youth Core is to broaden and strengthen the

Christian ministry by, with, and for young people in their conference. One goal which they adopted is to hold a series of three weekend leadership events which enable a core group of young people and adults to learn creative Christian leadership skills so that they are able to resource local church youth ministries and cluster gatherings of young people. Some elements which they see involved in creative Christian leadership skills are:

- To work together in team or co-leadership styles to support, enjoy and complement each other
- To understand some elements of group dynamics, leadership styles, skills in problem solving, interest assessment, and goal setting
- To know how to enable a group to help themselves and own a solution
- To strengthen one's commitment to God and the church

They hold a series of three weekend retreats which are attended by about thirty youth and adults. All make a commitment to attend all three weekends, to be available to resource other local churches as needed and to lead cluster events for churches in their area when possible. Because of the distance, people arrive at all hours and the total group often is not assembled until 11:00p.m. Thus, very little major programming is able to take place on Friday evenings.

The objectives for each of the three weekends are as follows:

Weekend I

Friday Evening
Objective: Do some initial, informal get-acquainted exercise, explore the camp setting and worship together.

Saturday Morning
Objectives: Get acquainted with each other and learn some

group building exercises and techniques. Clarify the purpose of the three weekends and why we are here. Emphasizing the intentional shift in leadership, all participants would be responsible to lead a segment by the end of the third training weekend.

Saturday Afternoon
Objectives: Acquaint the group with the faith exploration process and increase the awareness that we are here because we are children of God. Increase the comfort level for talking about our Christian faith.

Saturday Evening
Objectives: Outline different types of personalities. Discuss ways that these personalities work together in groups. Do exercises which brings out personality types and cooperation. Discuss motivations and hidden agendas which may be present in groups.

Sunday Morning
Objectives: Learn the structure of the United Church of Christ. Discover what being a part of the church means to us. Develop a statement of purpose for the Youth Core. Make plans and assignments for the next weekend.

Weekend II

Friday Evening
Objective: Give participants some information about leading groups and schedule leadership from the group for the remaining sessions.

Saturday Morning
Objective: Formulate a definition of youth ministry that is owned by the group and determine what issues and concerns should be faced by this ministry.

Saturday Afternoon
Objective: Explore the variety of resources that can be used in youth ministry, both by looking through the Youth Ministry Resources available and by challenging the creativity of the group.

Saturday Evening
Objectives: Give overview and summarize all the learnings that have taken place in the two weekends so far. Affirm the purposes and skill development of the group. In pairs, plan a program for a youth group meeting, a one-day workshop, a two-day retreat or a full-weekend retreat.

Sunday Morning
Objectives: Begin to identify individual strengths and planned leadership roles as participants present their designed programs. Negotiate how and when these decisions will be implemented.

Weekend III

Friday Evening
Objectives: Share experiences and key learnings from the programs led since the last meeting. Have the group respond and critique each presentation. Create a second design integrating both team learnings and group critique. Share revised plans.

Saturday Morning
Objectives: Review the various roles and functions of the local church, association and conference levels. Identify the boards and commissions where the youth and youth advocates might best contribute.

Saturday Afternoon
Objectives: Target specific membership on committees and commissions and propose nominations for these. Begin plans for youths' participation at the association and conference annual meetings.

Saturday Evening
Objectives: Develop a plan of action for Youth Presence. Decide step by step what needs to be done and a time line for doing it. Provide for shared leadership in accepting responsibility and clear lines of accountability (who needs to see what and when each step is accomplished). Be clear about how information will be shared with the Youth Team, as well as the local church, association and conference.

Sunday Morning
Objectives: In a celebrative style, look forward to the future with hope for success but be aware that the coming of the Kingdom is not entirely in our hands. Explore what each member would like to do from here and challenge all to be ministers and servants of God. Highlight the support of the Youth Team for each other and affirm individual talents. Close with songs and commissioning.

Note

1. The Planning Key Worksheet was designed jointly with Larry Golemon and Bernie C. Dunphy-Linnertz, and adapted.

CHAPTER NINE

Resources All Around Us

A resource is anything or anyone that can be used for a learning experience. Resources are, literally, all around us. Everywhere we turn.

Journal Jottings IX

Take a moment and jot down three new things you have learned this week: new information you may have acquired about your job, some studies, the world, a personal insight about yourself or a friend, your faith, a craft, etc.

Now think about where or from whom you learned it— from the newspaper, television, magazine, a good book, the person next door, a long talk with a friend, a teacher, or a prayer. These places and people and moments are all resources to you in some way.

What a wide universe is opened if we consider all those things which have been learning experiences for us. If we open up our eyes, ears, and awareness to the possibilities of resources that exist in our own backyards, there will be too many to use in a whole lifetime of ministry.

Journal Jottings X

Think about the people you know.
Pick out a person you know who may be particularly interesting. Now list out some possible talents or skills which you think that person has to share.
For example:

My mother

Sewing
Bookkeeping
Macrame
Wire art crafts
Crochet
Cooking
Piano
Camping skills
Income tax help
Solid Christian faith
Information on community
    health programs

Many people you know have several talents and skills, some you may not even be aware of, which they would be willing to tell about or demonstrate. These people are valuable resources.

Communities are abundant in trained people of all fields who would welcome an opportunity to be a part of your programming. Local church pastors or denominational judicatory staff are often available to give ideas and assistance also.

One often overlooked resource is the creativity which lies within all those who are part of your youth ministry group. Just as the wants and needs which give focus to your programming must come out of this group, so too can the creative ideas for building programs. The following exercises are two possible ways to bring out that creativity and share ideas.

From Mystery to Magic

Select a large number of items from your home and church. These could include:

dominos	record player	records of
toys	children's games	popular and
balloons	books	classical music
scenic slides	write-on slides	T shirts
rope	dictionary	light bulb
test papers	weather balloon	crayons
TV Guide	Bible	tape recorder
coloring books	cards	ladder
	play money	

Have these items arranged in random batches of about eight items each. Break the total group into small groups of four people and give each group a batch of eight items when they come in. Explain that these will be used later.

In the total group initiate a general discussion asking, "What are the major areas of interest and concern for teenagers today?" Generate a list of as many interest/concern areas as come up. Post these so they are visible to all. Then put them in order of priority. List the top six or eight areas of interest and concern. Post these. Possibilities may include: peer relations, relations with parents, sports, music, career choices, drugs/alcohol problems, competition, role stereotypes, etc.

The task of each small group is to plan a program based on one of these areas of interest or concern (one of their choosing), using at least two (or more) of the eight items their group was given. This program must be geared to a specific setting, such as a youth group meeting, weekend retreat, judicatory youth rally, ecumenical retreat, etc. Each group is given thirty minutes or more to design their program in as much detail as possible, outlining exactly how they will use the objects chosen, and what the goals of the program will be. At the end of the thirty minutes, each small group overviews their program for the total group.

One group of young people in Tennessee developed a very moving program about teenage suicide, using their items of a toy gun, a clothesline and a tape recorder. Other surprisingly innovative program ideas are stimulated just by brainstorming on possible uses of everyday objects.

Squared Away

Each person is given a blank sheet of 8x11 inch paper and a pencil. On the top half of the sheet, they are asked to number from one to five twice. On the bottom half they are to draw a large box divided into four parts. Each section of the box is to be labeled with a different adjective: Terrific, Pretty Good, Not Bad, and No Interest.

Each person is asked to list next to one set of numbers the five best things he or she ever did as part of a church group, school group, family, or group of friends. These might include camping trips, social trips, hayrides, summer camp, youth rallies, etc. On the other side each one lists the five most interesting learning/educational or service experiences she or he was ever involved in or heard about. These could be special work projects, college career days, trips to nursing homes, visits to juvenile courts or homes, etc.

The group is then asked to stand, circulate, and share experiences and ideas in this manner: Lorin greets Carol and shares one of his own experiences of ideas from either list. Carol then shares an idea from one of her lists with him. After

1.   1.

2.   2.

3.   3.

4.   4.

5.   5.

Terrific	Pretty Good
Not Bad	No Interest

listening to the idea or experience of Carol, Lorin writes it down in the box on his own sheet according to his level of interest in that idea. Carol does the same with the idea from Lorin. Thus, Lorin may say that going to the denominational annual conference meeting was one of his best experiences. Carol has a high level of interest in doing that so she writes "Going to denominational conference meeting" in her Terrific box. Carol's idea was to have a coffeehouse and invite youth from other churches. Lorin feels that this is a pretty good idea and writes it in his Pretty Good box. No names are recorded by the ideas. After their exchange, Carol and Lorin both move on to share new ideas with other people.

Everyone circulates and shares as many of their own ideas as possible with as many people as possible. This goes on for about fifteen minutes. The total group then comes back together. The ideas and experiences that people rated as "Terrific" and "Pretty Good" on their sheets are asked for and listed on newsprint. These are discussed and posted to be used later in the group's programming.

This is also a helpful method for sharing ideas among several groups.

Youth Ministry Resources

Multitudes of excellent books on all phases of youth ministry are also available. These books are available in your bookstore or can be ordered easily.

Everywhere there are resources. Stop, look and listen. Read, explore and check around. Challenge, create and have fun. Uncover the special gifts of those around you and give your own special gifts to them.

Often a recommended list of resources is provided by denominational offices. The following are selections from a much longer list compiled by the JED Youth staff. This list includes some of the more recent publications as well as those considered to be basic books for any youth ministry collection. (The prices indicated are subject to change.)

ABINGDON'S FOUNDATION SERIES: New Serendipity Series, by Lyman Coleman. Meets today's demand for more serious Bible study and in-depth discussion of life's problems. All courses have 7 sessions, and may be used individually as an elective or together as a complete course. May be ordered from Cokesbury Bookstores.

Self-Profile: The Me Nobody Knows deals with self-image, values, strengths, hang-ups, beliefs, dreams, and goals. 1981.
Leader, $4.95   Student, $1.25

Spiritual Basics: New Life in Christ deals with the difficulties and doubts often encountered in the Christian life. 1981.
Leader, $4.95   Student, $1.25

Body Building: Where Two or Three Are Gathered stresses the community of faith through such stories as the prodigal son and the wedding at Cana. 1981.
Leader, $4.95   Student, $1.25

Coping: Oh God, I'm Struggling deals with headaches, hassles, overload, failure, and starting over. 1981.
Leader, $4.95   Student, $1.25

My Calling: Here I Am, Lord emphasizes responsibility, accountability, and using one's God-given talents. 1980.
Leader, $4.95   Student, $1.25

ALTERNATIVE CELEBRATIONS CATALOGUE. This book offers creative alternatives for the commercialized celebrations in which many are involved. This is a very helpful resource in opening up the question of what we value in life. 1978. Available from Alternatives, 1924 East 3rd Street, Bloomington, In. 47401. $5.00.

BIBLE JOURNEYS, by Dick Orr and David L. Bartlett. Bible stories imaginatively retold in first-person narrative for senior high and older youth. Ideal for personal and group study of Christian growth. 1980. Judson Press, $4.95.

BUILDING AN EFFECTIVE YOUTH MINISTRY, by Glenn E. Ludwig. Concentrates on establishing a youth ministry "from scratch," with ideas tested and proven in several denominations. Includes organizing, selecting a leader, planning programs and publicity. 1979. Abingdon Press, $4.95.

CARING, FEELING, TOUCHING, Sidney Simon. This resource explores the importance of touching within families. This is a provacative resource suggesting the value of physical affection in preventing violence and sexual experimentation among adolescents. Argus, 1976. $2.25.

CATCHING THE RAINBOW: Total-Concept Youth Ministry, ed. J. David Stone. Volume 2 of the *Complete Youth Ministries Handbook*. Using the "rainbow" theme, writers from both Roman Catholic and Protestant traditions set forth refreshing ways of working with youth groups. Abingdon Press, 1981. $19.95.

CREATIVE YOUTH LEADERSHIP: For Adults Who Work with Youth, by Jan Corbett. Explains important skills needed for leadership development, plus tips on understanding youth, group experiences, use of resources, and teaching methods that work. Judson, 1977. $4.95.

DISCUSSION STARTERS FOR YOUTH GROUPS, by Ann Billups. Each volume contains material for 20 programs, with tear-out sheets and role-playing situations for groups of 3–5 youth. Discussion questions included. Judson Press, 1976.
Volume 1—$7.95
Volume 2—$7.95
Volume 3—$7.95

EXPERIMENTS IN GROWTH, Betsy Caprio. This book is action and activity oriented. The author presents a wide variety of experiences leading to spiritual growth. Ave Maria Press, 1976. $5.95.

EXPERIMENTS IN PRAYER, Betsy Caprio. This is a book of programmatic suggestions for encouraging active prayer within a youth group. Ave Maria Press, 1973. $3.95.

KEEP IN TOUCH: Prayers, Poems, Images and Celebrations by and for the Young, Herman C. Ahrens, Jr., editor. This is a collection of resources written by young people. Pilgrim Press, 1978. $4.95.

MUCH ADO ABOUT SOMETHING, Judy Fletcher. This resource packet explores the strengths and weaknesses of denominational youth ministry by use of a comparative study of independent youth ministries. Presbyterian Publishing House, $2.50.

THE NEW GAMES BOOK: PLAY HARD, PLAY FAIR, NO-BODY HURT, Andrew Fluegelman, editor. This collection of games is good for all ages, all size groups, and is lots of fun. It is a product of the New Games Foundation. Doubleday, $6.95.

PERSPECTIVES, by Ann Billups. A series of 35 exercises in values clarification. Common situations based on Christian faith are presented; youth must evaluate critically the 5 differing viewpoints in each. "Thoughtful and open-ended." Judson Press, $11.95.

RELIGIOUS EDUCATION MINISTRY WITH YOUTH, edited by D. Campbell Wyckoff and Don Richter. A report of a project sponsored by Princeton Theological Seminary. Includes information about today's youth, the condition of youth work in churches, existing youth programs of promise, and some essential elements in the future of youth ministry. Religious Education Press, 1982. $12.95.

RESPOND. A series of resource books for leaders of older youth, with a special section for use with junior highs. Gives practical advice, ideas, study suggestions. Includes help with planning and using a variety of methods-discussion, surveys, dramatic skits, choral readings, simulations. Judson Press, 1972.
Volume 2, edited by Janice J. Corbett. Resource sections on the Bible, the church, social issues, Eastern religions, meditation,

SEVENTY-SEVEN WAYS OF INVOLVING YOUTH IN THE CHURCH, Richard Bimler. This book includes background, designs, exercises, and leadership information for helping youth become a vital part of the church's ministry. Concordia Press, 1976. $3.95.

YOUTH ELECT SERIES. Resources of Christian Education: Shared Approaches, Living the Word. For use in weekly fellowship meetings, retreats, or camps and conferences. May be ordered from your denominational curriculum service.
Idealog: Creative Ideas for Older Youth—Anthology of program ideas for study, worship, recreation. 1979. $4.95

A Matter of Life and Death—Christian perspective on death. 1977. $1.75

Exploring Other World Religions—A look at the great faiths of humanity. 1980. $1.75

The Search for Intimacy—Six sessions on love, sexuality, and commitment. 1981. $2.25

Act in Faith—Living the Word through drama. 1983. $2.25

YOUTH MAGAZINE. This is a contemporary quarterly publication for high school youth. Cartoons, interviews, poetry, real life stories and ideas for programs are included. A helpful CE:SA resource for youth and those who care about youth. Available from your denominational curriculum service. Individual subscriptions, $10.00 year, Three or more to the same address $7.60 year.

YOUTH: A MANUAL FOR CE:SA, David Ng. A basic youth ministry resource for church school teachers and fellowship leaders. The best section is on adolescent development and teaching adolescents. Geneva Press, 1977. $2.25.

YOUTH MANUAL, Jill Senior. This 95-page looseleaf notebook presents a comprehensive overview of practical youth ministry. Youth ministry is presented from a theological and developmental perspective. There are good sections on planning and resources. PCUS $5.00.

YOUTH MANUAL UPDATE. This update strengthens the YOUTH MANUAL in the areas of youth leadership, empowerment, and includes four new models for youth ministry. A section on the history of youth ministry in the PCUS has also been included. PCUS $1.50.

YOUTH MINISTRY IN THE SMALL CHURCH. A very helpful booklet comprised of reprints from STRATEGY magazine. It is a good resource for evaluation and planning Presbyterian Publishing House, $1.95.

YOUTH MINISTRY: The Gospel and the People, by Gabriel Fackre and Jan Chartier. The importance to youth of a loving, caring, environment in the church, implications of the gospel message for youth, plus creative program ideas. Judson Press, 1979. $5.95.

YOUTH MINISTRY: The New Team Approach, by Ginny Ward Holderness. Popular author of youth ministry resources suggests having a team share the load of youth ministry, rather than "burning out" one or two individuals. "Sound and helpful . . . should be on any new youth bibliography." John Knox Press, 1981. $9.95.

YOUTH WORKER'S SUCCESS MANUAL, by Shirley Pollock. Make that teen energy work *for* your church, with these 100 proven ideas for getting youth more involved in church activities. Abingdon Press, 1978. $3.95.